DESTINY by CHOICE

Thom Lemmons

QUESTAR PUBLISHERS, INC.
Sisters, Oregon

DESTINY BY CHOICE

© 1989 by Thom Lemmons
Published by Questar Publishers, Inc.

Printed in the United States of America

ISBN 0-945564-13-9

Cover design: Al Mendenhall

FOREWORD

If you could ask Isaac what he felt as he saw his father Abraham raise the knife to kill his son...

If Ruth were at your table telling you her story...

If Joseph were to reveal to you the pain and passion of raising the Christ-child...

If Lazarus had kept a journal of his encounter with Jesus and his journey through death...

If all these mysteries were made known to us, perhaps they might well read like the fascinating sketches in *DESTINY BY CHOICE*. Thom Lemmons and Questar Publishers have done us a favor. By wedding scholarship with creativity they have given birth to some sparkling glimpses into biblical hearts.

You'll see Adam longing to be a better father...Zaccheus eyeing Christ from the sycamore tree...the wedding hosts staring at the empty wine jugs. You'll see the characters of Scripture that make Scripture so real. And you'll see them with new insight as Thom skillfully suggests thoughts you'd never entertained.

It is with great joy that I commend this writer and his thoughts to you. You'll soon see, as I saw, that this book was authored by a man whose love for words is exceeded only by his love for God.

This is Thom's first book, and for our sake, I pray it's the first of a hundred.

MAX LUCADO

ACKNOWLEDGMENTS

I HAVE BEEN BLESSED with the help of some wonderful and understanding people as I struggled to give life to the child you hold in your hands. I would be most remiss if I did not acknowledge their contributions:

Cheryl, my wife, my other self — who never doubted (even when I did!);

Mother and Dad — who gave me two gifts: a love for reading, and the knowledge of the Author of Life;

Max Lucado — a friend and mentor, who gave encouragement in this project at a critical juncture;

Bo Whitaker — my first editor, and a dear brother;

Dr. Ian Fair, Dean of the College of Biblical Studies at Abilene Christian University — his gracious support was vital;

Dr. John Willis, Professor of Bible at Abilene Christian — whom I thank for shepherding me and sharing his many insights into the Old Testament;

Dr. Thomas Geer, Assistant Professor of Greek and New Testament at Abilene Christian — to whom I'm grateful for helping me clarify my thinking about the Apostle John;

Dr. Carroll Osburn, Professor of Greek and New Testament at Abilene Christian — his brilliant exposition of the historical milieu of first-century Palestine made the Gospel of Mark come alive for me;

Dr. Jack Welch, Professor of English at Abilene Christian — I thank him for persuading me I might have something to say;

The Church at South Fifth & Highland in Abilene, Texas — I thank the elders and the family for nurturing me, challenging me, and using me. In their care, I have grown;

Thomas Womack, Don Jacobson, and the whole Questar family — whom I thank for taking a chance on an unknown quantity. And more than that, I thank them for their prayers.

I am also deeply indebted to F. F. Bruce's excellent volume *New Testament History.* To it I owe much of the historical underpinning of "Journal," "And We Beheld His Glory," and "Eulogy."

This work would not have existed without the aid of these people. To the extent the book succeeds, they, along with God, deserve the credit.

INTRODUCTION

OUR GOD, all-powerful though He is, has left one corner of the universe entirely in our control — the decision whether to serve Him or not. Tiny though this crack in the wall may be, it is sufficient to admit all the demons of hell into the garden.

There can be room in a human life for but one god. We must choose. And we must do it entirely on our own. Having once done so, our god then assists us in the subsequent choices, if we listen to its voice. When we do not like the answer a particular god gives us — then we can always find another whose bidding suits us better. I see a great many people who seem to be forever bouncing back and forth between gods. I have done a bit of bouncing myself.

This book is about people and choices. Or, perhaps more properly, The Choice. The characters in these stories are people I have met in the pages of the Bible. I am persuaded that human nature has not changed much in the past four thousand years or so. When I read the Bible, I am forever smitten by how similar these folk are to me and to others I have known. They have the same desires, the same urges, the same foibles, the same occasional greatness as anyone you might encounter on the street today. As a brother named Stanley Shipp once said, Bible characters are "just plain old folks who happened to be standing around when the Bible got written."

Perhaps a word of caution is in order. I make no claim to be a Bible scholar. This little book is not intended as a commentary. I have ascribed thoughts, motives and actions to persons who lived thousands of years and several cultures away from my experience. While I would never intentionally promote a view of events essentially contrary to Scripture, I have painted these vignettes with colors different than those you or someone else may have chosen. If these imaginative excursions into the past please you, or hold up God's will to you at a slightly different angle, or offer you some new, helpful perspective — I have met my aim.

My prayer is that each person who reads these lines will understand the inevitability of choice. For by our choices we are measured.

Know that the Lord Himself is God;
it is He who has made us and not we ourselves;
we are His people
and the sheep of His pasture.

Psalm 100:3

DESTINY by CHOICE

Fathers & Sons

WHEN HE was being born, I was afraid. I was afraid the woman would die, and I would be left alone. More than anything, I feared being alone. We had been cut off once before. And now, to be without even her voice...

But she did not die. She looked up at me, the pain-sweat running off her face. She held him at her breast like a treasure, like a long-sought vindication. She said, "The Lord has helped us get a man-child." So we called him Cain. Our acquisition, our Cain had arrived.

For a while he was as helpless as a baby sparrow fallen from the nest. He changed quickly though. It seemed no time had passed before he was digging little garden plots with child-sized tools. He was fascinated by anything green and growing. Soon he proved his ability to nurture earth, bringing some fresh herb or ripe fruit for his mother's cooking pot at the end of each day.

Though I watched him grow, I could not fathom how quickly

it happened. Just sitting and watching him dig the soil or
climb a tree or taste a fruit for the first time — I was enchant-
ed. It reminded me of the time Before...when everything was
new. In his joyful concentration on each new discovery, I saw
my former wonder.

When Abel was born, I was more excited than afraid. And
before he was a year old I could tell he was not inclined the
same as Cain. Instead of heading toward the fields to gather
and till with his mother, he was drawn by the animals. And
the animals seemed to like Abel. I was glad, because I had
always needed help milking the goats. He reminded me of
one of the kids himself, the way he laughed and tumbled
headfirst, wrestling with the pups or chasing a straying goose.
Watching Cain and Abel play filled me with renewed
hope. Their laughter — their lives — were my redemption.

As they got older, the trouble between them started.
Maybe it was my fault, for always taking Abel with me into
the pastures. Maybe Cain decided I loved Abel better. The
thing that haunts me is...maybe I did. I needed another friend
so desperately, and I wanted to find him in my boys. I wanted
to tell them about the time Before...

I tried to talk about it, but sometimes the feelings jammed
in my throat, and the pain of remembering forced the water
from my eyes and made the words tremble on my lips.
Watching me, Cain often seemed uncomfortable, as though it
shamed him to see my weakness. Usually he would walk
away to the fields or talk to his mother.

But Abel would stay beside me. It was the animals with

me, perhaps; they were a comfort to him while I choked down my grief, and when I was ready to talk again, he was there. Abel listened. Perhaps his brother saw this, and didn't understand.

However it was, the quarrels intensified. Abel complained about Cain throwing rocks at his goats when they got close to the garden. And Cain griped that I did nothing about the animals ruining his crops. "Abel is your favorite," he whined.

Things got worse, and I couldn't find the words to make them better. I just didn't know the words.

Eventually, their enmity deepened into a cold war of silences and grudges. I wonder now: Did Cain feel the same inward pull I had felt, in the time Before? Did he feel the choice burning in his chest? Did he hear the footsteps of One who would expose his cowering soul? Or was he numb to everything, as his scalding anger threw him headlong into darkness?

I try to think about it, to understand what made him do it. But perhaps my own vision is too scarred and blinded by regret for the choices I've made.

When Cain realized what he'd done that day, his first impulse was to put Abel's bloodied corpse into the ground; to sow his brother like a seed. What harvest did he hope to reap from such a dreadful planting?

Hard as it was for me, I think their mother suffered more, seeing her son bring such blood-evil into the world. Part of her died with Abel. Cain's blow struck her too.

And me? I lost both sons that day. I lost the tomorrows I should have had with them — the friendship we could have shared, the things I never got to say. I lost the redemption I thought was mine. I just didn't know the words.

Still I find no words, no message of my own, to comfort my ache. With nowhere else to turn, I listen again to the Lord's last words when we were with Him. For so long after that wrenching day I had wished to forget them, but could not, and now I know I am glad I cannot. I remember them, letting the words rush over my mind like the rivers we knew in the Garden.

They speak of pain, enmity, cursing. There is always sweatful toil to bear, always an enemy at our heels. But there will also be a day to crush him. And in that day I find my hope.

P RACTICING ON A distant, slender young juniper, I was shooting my bow not far from our tents, As I drew the last arrow from my quiver, for some reason I thought of all the arrows my father had whittled for me since teaching me how to shoot. He had made this bow for me as well, and as I gripped it firmly, I was sure I would be using it for many years.

I released the shot — a hit — and had just begun walking to retrieve the arrows when I saw Father coming out to me. His steps were slow. I stopped, and as he came closer I saw that his eyes were red.

He said only, "We must go far away and make a sacrifice to God. You must come too."

I put aside the bow, and began helping him gather the wood we would need.

Early the next morning we got up, and he told me to say goodbye to Mother. He didn't come with me when I went in to kiss her. "Take good care of your father," she told me.

Two of our men came with us, and together we walked for three days. On the first morning I asked Father where we were going, but he wouldn't answer or look at me; his quiet, forward stare made me feel a little afraid. I asked him nothing more, content to remember our many journeys together when I was younger, when on the way he would describe for me in detail the places we were to see, as well as tell me stories. Often the stories were about what I would be someday. He used to ask what I would do when I was a father myself, and had a curious son who asked questions all the time. Then he would laugh, pick me up and toss me in the air, and tell me again of God's promise that I would someday be a father of many.

The third day I saw him stop and gaze intently at a hilltop ahead of us. His face looked as if he were listening to someone. The rest of us stopped behind him. Then he turned, told the men to stay back, and lifted the wood off the donkey. He took my hand and we started climbing.

I was confused. We had come a long way to give God a sacrifice, but had no animals except the donkey we left below. "Where is the lamb?" I asked.

This time he answered, but I had never before heard such a strange sound to his voice. "God will provide a lamb for us," he said.

I felt like running away and hiding, but I didn't. We kept climbing.

The top was quiet and bare and rocky, and I could see all around. I could even see the men and the donkey in the valley below, looking like clay toys.

My father laid down the bundle of wood and asked me to help him gather rocks for the altar. I knew what to do; I had helped him build altars before.

Carefully we laid the rocks beside and on top of one another. I ventured to speak again: "This must be an important altar, since God had us make a three-day trip to come here." He was silent again; I looked and saw his tears.

I helped him arrange the wood on the altar — carefully, so the fire would be hot enough. I was putting on the last piece when I felt him grip my shoulder from behind. My first thought was that he wanted to wrestle, as we so often had done in fun. Instinctively I twisted my shoulder from his grip, laughing a little, and turned around with my arms extended. He grabbed them, and suddenly began tying them with a leather strap — so tightly that it hurt. Frozen with the fear of unknowing, I could only watch as he then tied my legs. I couldn't move.

He picked me up, then laid me on top of the wood, just as I had seen him do with a lamb — with a gentle but decisive motion. From his belt he took out the knife he always used for sacrifices. His mouth was open and his lips were moving, but no sounds came out. Again I saw his tears.

I felt the wood pressing painfully into my flesh. One word — *Father?* — was formed in my throat, but I could not speak. I saw him lift the knife, slowly at first, then suddenly jerk it high above him.

I closed my eyes and turned my head. All I could hear

was the thunder of my heart, pounding as if it would split open within me.

It seemed such a long time before I opened my eyes again and turned toward him. He was looking down the hill. I followed his gaze, and saw a ram tangled in the bushes, caught by its horns. My father looked back at me, and I searched his eyes. I was finally able to give voice to my cry: *"Father?"*

He nodded...then fell to his knees, sobbing.

On the way home, fresh memories kept blazing up in my mind — of our long, silent embrace after he cut me loose and helped me off the wood...of my shudder at the sight of blood coming from the ram's throat slit open with the knife...of our spoken prayers of thanksgiving welling up from our hearts while the sacrifice burned...of the moments soon afterward when the sky turned strangely dark, and my father again heard the Voice from heaven, repeating cherished words of promise about his offspring — *like stars in the sky...sand on the seashore...through them all nations will be blessed...*

As we now walked, I kept hearing deep echoes of the things my father always told me about God: *He is good. He keeps His promises. Everything He does is for a reason. Always listen to Him.* Now I wanted more than ever to listen to Him, because I wanted to *understand.*

But I didn't understand. *Father — why?* Would it ever make sense? Did it make sense to him?

"Son—" His voice startled me, stilling the storm in my

thoughts. "You must never forget how God provided a sacrifice."

I won't, Father. I didn't understand — how could I? But I knew I would never forget.

A Tale of Two Grasshoppers

THE SWEATY ODOR of nervous anticipation permeated the predawn darkness in Moses' tent. Twelve chosen men stood before him, twelve tribal leaders who were to reconnoiter the land of God's promise. Fear and duty skirmished across their faces — leaving their traces in edgy glances, flared nostrils, and frequent swallows.

Unnoticed, I crouched in the corner, watching them. I saw my father, young and strong, take his place among the men.

A deaf-mute would have sensed the tension. The long, dry march of our people was to end. Our goal was within reach. We were at the portal of Canaan.

Doubtless the anxiety of the men had something to do with being called into the presence of Moses. They knew unpleasant things sometimes happened to those who attracted the leader's disfavor; even members of his own family were not immune.

Of the twelve, only Joshua the Ephraimite seemed steady. He

who had been at Moses' right hand, he who had served him as a son, seemed eager to be about the business of conquest. The steel in his eyes glinted as he leaned forward to listen. So intent was he, he almost pulled the leader's thoughts from his mind before they were spoken.

Moses gave the twelve their dangerous commission: to survey the land, to observe the disposition of its people, to explore its borders, and to bring back a sampling of its fruits. Then he placed his hands on the head of each man, blessing and conferring the protection of the Almighty upon the mission. When Moses reached Joshua, the older man embraced the younger for a moment, two moments. Joshua turned, and with the others slipped out into the darkness to begin the ascent into the Negev.

In the forty days my heroes were away, I died a thousand deaths. I imagined every conceivable mishap, and invented dozens of others. Each day, as my mother arose, I pestered her with questions: "What tidings of the Twelve? Have they sent back word? Do you suppose they have been discovered? Will the tribes of Canaan descend upon us?" Forty interminable days she shook her head at my impetuous queries. Forty eternities I tortured myself with fancies more vivid than reality.

At last the day came. A shout raced through the camp on a hundred tongues: "They return! The Twelve return!" From the tabernacle outward to the most distant tents, word of our spies' return came rippling across Kadesh like a drumroll. The news pulled the wind out of my breast, thrust my heart into my throat as I rushed toward the meeting place by Moses' dwelling. I was surrounded by scores of others who were running, their feet as irresistibly drawn as mine.

Thinking back, I recall the half-worried, half-joyful countenances of the people as they went to hear word of the Promised Land. Yet, in the end, worry betrayed joy.

The Twelve were already assembled along the rocky height behind the leader's tent. Moses rapidly picked his way up the steep path. The people crowded against the very edge of the place where the heroes stood, and more came in behind, until there was a huge press from the throng. Agility was required to avoid being trampled in the confusion. The place abutted a rocky cliff, forming a natural theater that served to amplify the voice of any who addressed the multitude.

As I strained forward to the front, I expected to see my father's arms raised in victory with the others. But the twelve men were arguing among themselves. Joshua and one other — Caleb of Judah — appeared to be withstanding a vigorous scolding administered by the other ten, my father among them. I saw Father's face grow red as he and the others flung their arms in wide, angry gestures.

Moses reached them, and their anger subsided, but still they muttered among themselves. Then quiet fell, broken only by the shuffling of feet and the cry of a baby.

"Speak up," Moses said, his voice rebounding from the cliffs behind and about him, "you who have gone into the land. Tell me and your people about the country promised to us by the Almighty Lord."

The twelve men looked nervously at one another. Finally my father took a few halting steps forward. He cleared his throat. Looking away from Moses and over the heads of the people, he said, "The land is...it's a good land, a fertile land. But the people who dwell there are bigger and taller than we. They live in large, strong cities with walls halfway to heaven. They have mighty warriors among them, and — and we saw giants there!"

He began saying more, but the swelling chorus of groans and exclamations from below drowned out his voice.

Those around me looked at each other, some disbelieving, some smugly frowning, their worst fears satisfyingly confirmed. As the clamor gained in volume, another voice rang out above the dismayed multitude. I scrambled for a better position to see who it was.

"No! No! You must not listen to this!" So insistent was Caleb's tone that the mob grew uneasily quiet, redirecting its attention to him. He stood with clenched fists, glaring defiantly at the ten who stood across from them. With Joshua at his side, Caleb strode to the edge of the high place. Looking first at Moses and Joshua, then at the people below, he spoke in a clear, strong voice.

"The land to which the Lord brings us flows with milk and honey!" He reached down at his feet, tearing a cluster of large grapes from a huge bunch strung on a pole, and shook the fruit above his head as he held the crowd with his eyes. "And there are pomegranates and figs as well! These are the fruits of Canaan, which the Lord has promised to give us — if only we will take it. And we *can!*"

I looked behind me, expecting nods of renewed confidence and confirmation, but only scowls and downcast faces met my smile. Could they hear no voice but that of their own doubts? Were they deaf to all but words of doom?

Another of the ten thrust himself in front of Caleb, and turned to the people: "The land devours its inhabitants!" he shouted. "It is a wonder we returned alive. Do you wish to fight hand-to-hand with giants? Can grasshoppers such as we bring down the mighty Nephilim?"

Louder groans came from the crowd, their consternation visibly growing by the instant. Another of the ten seized the moment, crying out: "We cannot go in to be mangled by the blood weapons we have witnessed with our own eyes. We *will not!*"

A quick roar of assent ripped through the crowd.

"NO!" shouted Moses, pointing his staff like a spear at the hearts of the attackers, and holding it there until all was silent. Anger crackled outward from him like lightning, and I flinched from his burning eyes. Though the ten were maddened with fear, their resolve crumbled before the wrath that washed outward from Moses in a palpable wave. Grumbling, they withdrew, though not without threatening looks at Joshua and Caleb.

The people wandered away to their tents, ruefully chewing their cuds of woe.

That night, I watched as men came to my father's tent, their eyes shifting this way and that. From my place in the corner, I listened incredulously as they asked, in low, sniveling voices, whether we should choose another leader who would take us back to Egypt.

Surely my father would never turn back to slavery; surely he would look into the sordid faces of these men and curse them. My boyish will to conquer was inflamed. I wanted to shout down these cowards, to drive them from our tent, to flay them alive with the flashing blades of my indignation.

They waited for my father's reply. From behind him, I saw his shoulders sag. Finally, I saw his head nod silently in agreement...

I stared at his back in wordless disbelief. In a sudden rush of horror, I felt hatred for my father. I clenched my jaw against the wail of anguish clawing at the back of my throat, and slipped out of the tent into the solitude of darkness.

That night was a bad one for me. Always before, the strong backs of my parents had fended the desiccating winds of uncertainty from striking me with their full force. Until now, I never doubted their ability to clear the path for me, to point me in the right way. But with his shrug of defeat, the shelter of my father was forever denied me. I now faced alone a perilous, ambiguous future. I raged within at my father for his inability to see what was — to my child's eyes — perfectly clear.

I wandered the camp like a lost soul. At every doorway, in every shadow, I overheard despairing sighs, conspiratorial whispers. I tasted a wrongness in the mood of our people, a foul stench polluting the whole camp. For the first time in my short life, I was truly alone. I did not have words for the cross-currents in my breast, and I have not learned them since. A lad of only some twelve summers, I fought with my own angel that night.

At dawn I squatted listlessly on my heels in our tent door, idly tossing pebbles at a clump of weeds a few paces away. I felt my father's eyes on me, but I did not look at him or acknowledge his presence. Sensing my bitterness, perhaps, he squatted before me. I could no longer decently ignore him. Reluctantly, I raised my eyes to his.

"If we go in, it will mean bloodshed and horror." He stopped, waiting for my reply. I kept quiet, and looked away.

"Fathers will be murdered, mothers and children taken as slaves. It is your welfare I consider. You must understand! Don't you see?"

A long silence ached between us, until I spoke. "But Caleb and Joshua —"

"Hah, Caleb and Joshua! Are they the only men sent to spy out the land? Do you believe it is only a fable that giants live there? Yours is a world of imaginary battles and fanciful games, but it is I who must draw the sword against the armies of Canaan. When the Philistines come against us with war chariots, do you suppose Joshua and Caleb can slay *them* with clever words? No, it's time you learned to face reality, my son. It's time you looked at the world through a man's eyes, instead of a child's."

I felt a scalding tide rising in my chest. I leapt to my feet and raced madly away, leaving my father crouched in the doorway, staring after.

Toward mid-morning I heard a commotion. Angry voices erupted in the direction of the cliffs. I raced among the tents of the Levitical compound toward the meeting place and the dwellings of Moses and Aaron.

As I drew near, a crowd of shouting men boiled out into the clearing. They bore down on the leader's tent, pushing Caleb and Joshua in their midst. Hearing the noise, Moses appeared at his doorway, followed by his brother. Both men looked drawn and tired, and I knew they, too, had not slept.

The mob swelled to the doorway, and like waves casting driftwood ashore, pressed Joshua and Caleb before them.

"We will have none of the suicidal ravings of these two!" someone shouted.

Caleb instantly shouted back, his voice half pleading, half protesting: "If God is pleased with us — if we do not lose faith in Him — He will surely give us wine from vines we did not plant, honey from hives we did not tend. God is with us! We should go up into the land, just as He has instructed us, and take it!"

Another frantic voice rang out from the crowd: "Would you have our children serve as concubines and eunuchs to the Jebusites and the Philistines? Do you wish your own flesh to be sword fodder for the sons of Anak?"

Now Joshua spoke up: "Have you forgotten so soon what mighty acts the Lord has already performed on our behalf? Is the Red Sea crossing so dim in your memories that you now doubt His strength? Is there a man here who has forgotten the taste of the quail and the manna? Have we not already gained victory over the armies of Pharaoh and the Amalekites by the arm of the Lord? Why shouldn't we be able to go in and take this land the Lord has prepared for us?"

A sneer arose: "The Amalekites are a rabble of nomadic herdsmen, not an entrenched people with strongholds!"

I felt my heart skip as I awaited Joshua's reply. At length, he smiled and pointed southwest, toward Egypt.

"The other spies have spoken of God's chosen as grasshoppers. So be it. Do you remember the locusts He brought against Pharaoh? Are we less mighty than they?"

I felt my whole being flush with pride at the way he threw the naysayer's words back in his teeth. But the crowd was unmoved. "Away with these fools!" some of them cried. "We will not listen to these madmen!" A few of them sprang up and grasped Caleb and Joshua, throwing them roughly to the ground at Moses' feet, but pausing before doing anything more. Joshua and Caleb looked up at Moses.

I watched the leader for some sign of his next action. For ten long breaths Moses stood glaring at the men. Then he sank slowly to his knees. He grasped the neck of his tunic and ripped it apart. A mournful wail emanated from his soul as he raised his eyes to heaven and clawed the dust with his hands.

The rebels had expected anything from Moses — except grief. They staggered back from Joshua and Caleb, unnerved by his reaction.

By now, Aaron, too, was kneeling on the ground, rocking to and fro, groaning and ripping his garments. The mob backed away, dropping the stones they had been nervously handling. Their anger and fear were less passionate than their awe of Moses and his reputation. Caleb and Joshua mingled their voices in the weeping.

I was numb. How could our painful journey be climaxed by this display of cowardly outbursts, and four solitary, brave men weeping in the dust?

Then, from the tabernacle, a glow dimmed the mid-morning sun as thunder rumbled suddenly across the settlement. I crouched behind a rock, but peeked out to see Moses walking to the tabernacle, his face glowing in its light, his eyes wide with wonder.

The terrible stabs of light and thunder went on for hours. At last I dared to crawl from my cover and stagger away, dragging my emotions behind me like a block of granite.

When I arrived home, my family still cowered in our tent with their arms over their heads, though the Voice by then had grown silent. Dazed and exhausted, I collapsed face down upon my pallet.

I was awakened by my father shaking my shoulder. "Arise, son," he was saying. "Moses has summoned us."

A leaden band tightened about my chest. Fearing the words I would hear, I traced in my father's eyes the same dread that shackled me. Still, we could not stay away.

In the light of dusk, we saw the men of Israel drifting in by clans and families, coming to the place of counsel. We took our place among them. Moses stood on the rock with Aaron on his left, Joshua and Caleb on his right. He leaned upon his staff like a man who had taken a mortal wound. From time to time he wavered, grasping Joshua's shoulder to steady himself.

Presently he looked out over the assembly, drawing a deep, quivering breath.

"People of Israel!" he began. "This is what the Almighty, the Lord of Hosts, says:

" 'How long will this people rebuke me? After all the wonders and signs I have performed among them, *how long will they refuse to believe?*

" 'Because they have seen My hand, have heard My voice, and have eaten at My table, and still have not believed, this unbelieving generation will not be spared. Every man and woman who has reached twenty years of age will perish in

♦

the desert, and never see the land I promised on oath to their fathers. They will not enter the land of promise, because they doubted My strength and My love. Of all the sons of Israel who are of a score years or more, only Joshua, son of Nun, and Caleb the son of Jephunneh will I allow to enter the land, for these two believed in Me.

" 'As for the rest of the people, they shall wander in the wilderness forty years, until the faithless generation has utterly perished...' "

The words went on, but I heard no more. Forty years more to wander — more than three of my lifetimes! To be so close, yet denied...my soul searched without success for order in the chaos of my heart.

That night we ate a supper of bitterness, dipped our bread in a bowl of acrid silence. I looked at my father — his eyes stared away, across the bleak landscape of Sinai, seeking his grave among the wastes.

He shrank before my gaze. I could see his life already ebbing, as he stood under the Almighty's wrath. The fore-knowledge of his fate — empty years of wandering, a hopeless wait — haunted his face, and leached his will to live.

My love for him battled with resentment for the trial his generation had brought upon me. I was a casualty of the war between innocence and reality. Trying to understand my own pain, I was helpless to comprehend his.

The darkness in my father crept out of his eyes, filling the tent, overwhelming the light from the fire. My mother bustled about in voiceless desperation, occupying herself with mundane household chores as a bar to the fear pressing its cold weight upon us. Even my baby sister ceased her usually tireless babble, crouching in a corner of the tent, watching us all with eyes older than her years.

The criers came around that evening, announcing our imminent departure. Soon we would begin our long retreat from the threshold of our inheritance.

I questioned my father openly. I asked him how it was that he, a chosen leader of Israel, could so disbelieve in the might of our God as to tacitly consent to the rebellion for which we were being punished. I flung my questions at him with the heedless haughtiness of idealistic youth. I cared not whether he ever answered me; indeed, I hardly expected any response. With my angry interrogation the chasm between us grew wider, his dark silence deeper.

Then, suddenly, he rounded upon me in rage. He clouted me in the ear so hard that I fell to the ground, stunned.

"You know a great deal, don't you?" he shouted, his face a purpling mask. I cowered beneath his fury.

In the morning, my father and the other nine naysayers among the twelve spies were found dead on their pallets. I helped bury him that day, then shouldered my pack and prepared to begin this journey with no destination.

Invisible walls had grown overnight, dividing parent and child. Together, yet alone, we faced the hot winds as we were led mercilessly away from Canaan's borders.

We would learn to live with death.

I STOOD on the banks of the Jordan at last, watching with tears as the Levites bore the Ark across the dry riverbed. My sons and grandsons stood beside me. I suppose they thought I wept for joy at the crossing into Canaan, and I did...but I also wept for my father, who was unable to believe in this day.

Once humiliated by his sin, I had come face to face with my own iniquity, too late regretting the proud words with which I had flayed him on his last day. So soon I saw people my age defile themselves with the whores of Moab, seduced by Balaam's sorcery into lustful disobedience. No generation is immune from poor choices.

But I also witnessed faith in the wilderness. Joshua and Caleb had seemed immune to the ravages of those years. Other men and women shriveled and perished, but these two became hardier, tougher. They drew sustenance and strength from a never-failing source. They could walk as far, see as keenly, fight as hard as any man my age.

Led by the example of these two grasshoppers, we would enter the land...and take it.

Wives & Daughters

LAPIDOTH SQUINTED from the dark tent doorway into the mid-morning brightness. A lone palm tree leaned over the muddy *wadi* at the center of this small valley in the flinty hills of Ephraim. A knot of petitioners gathered about the tree, some squatting, some standing, all waiting for the appearance of the judge.

The judge. His wife. Lapidoth sighed and let the goatskin flap fall. He turned and shuffled back to the tiny flame that licked feebly at a few charred twigs in a small depression at the center of the tent.

"They gather," he mumbled in the general direction of his wife, who sat staring at the fire. "You had best go to them."

"Yes, I know. I will go. It is time." She bowed her head, silently mouthed a prayer, then rose and stood with shoulders stooped, staring at the ground. Gradually she straightened, turned to the door, drew the flap aside and went out.

Lapidoth, still regarding the place his wife had vacated, sighed again. "O, Lord God," he finally intoned in a quavering voice, "why did You choose my wife? Why does Your heavy hand lie upon Deborah?"

The morning wore into the heat of the day and beyond as Deborah sat beneath the palm tree. Here was a disagreement about the sale of a donkey, there a dispute over a betrothal. This one petitioned for the use of a certain well, that one sought justice for a kinslaying. Patiently she listened, discerning the merits of each complaint.

And, as always, there were cries for relief from Jabin's oppression:

"He garnishes for himself the best of the flock and leaves us only the poor and sick."

"His general, Sisera the Hittite, drives his chariots through the midst of my herds, turning not to the left or right, and wantonly maims and mauls my beasts."

"When will our God save us from his hand? When?"

When indeed? She had no answer, no comfort for them. Long now had she beseeched the Lord's salvation from the hand of Jabin, but received silence in reply. Clearly, His time had not yet come. When would He speak? She could not say.

Toward evening, as the sunset gilded the surrounding crags and made them almost beautiful, the supplicants began to drift away. Deborah noticed a young woman still kneeling, peering intently at her, clearly desiring to speak to her. Going to her and laying her hand gently upon the girl's upturned cheek, the judge asked, "What do you seek, my child? It is evening and I must rest. Should you not go to your own home?"

"Wise one, the Lord has laid a burden upon my heart."

"Speak, then, daughter."

"I have come to wait here with you for the deliverance of Israel." The young woman's eyes glistened with intensity, and the words caught in her throat as she spoke.

Deborah looked carefully, deeply into her eyes. "What is your name, child?"

"I am Jael, wife of Heber of the Kenites."

A moment more the judge regarded her, then turned away. She closed her eyes, listening for the Voice within her that had been silent for so many years.

Again she faced Jael. "Why do you involve yourself? There is no feud between your husband's house and Jabin."

"Nevertheless, the Lord's spirit burns within me, and I cannot rest quiet among my people. I could do nothing else than seek you, for He would not let me be still." She bowed her head apologetically. "I do not explain well..."

"Well enough, my child," interrupted the older woman, patting Jael's shoulder and looking away into the distance. "I understand better than you know. Better than you could ever know." A silent moment passed, as the deepening evening shadows crawled catlike along the rocky ground.

"Stand up, Jael," commanded the judge presently, coming to a decision. "I have seen you, and I have heard your words. Now here is what you must do: Go back north to your home, and to you husband's tent. In the day the Lord God needs you, know that He will find you there. Do you understand?

Jael stared into Deborah's fatigued face. Slowly, hesitantly, she nodded.

"Yes...yes, I think so."

"Good. Now go. And remember this," she admonished, as the young woman turned to leave. "It is a hard thing to be a vessel in His hand...and a blessed thing. Do not forget."

Thoughtfully, Jael turned and began down the path. Deborah stood and watched her until the dusk shrouded her form in shadow.

Lapidoth watched quietly from the darkness as his wife entered and slumped onto her couch, holding her face in her hands. After a moment, he broke off a piece of the hard, round *matzah* loaf he held, eased over to Deborah and offered it to her.

"You should eat. You haven't taken nourishment all day."

A smile of appreciation momentarily dispelled the numb weariness in her face. She took it from him, and began to eat.

He thought of his wife as he had known her in their younger days. Wistfully he recalled her dark, flashing eyes; the way she tossed her beautiful long hair during their playful arguments. He remembered the soft glow on her face as she cradled their children in her arms. His chest tightened as he pictured again her doe-eyed look of pride and love, reserved for him alone, when they embraced.

Now he was afraid too much had changed, and still was changing. The children, of course, had long since left, but her care for them had been replaced by the awesome responsibilities of judgeship which the Lord God had laid upon her. Naturally it had altered her, matured her. But he feared also that something within her had become inaccessible to him.

Lapidoth could see it now, as she sat, completely spent, on her couch. All day she had listened, had decided, had arbitrated disputes and accepted the burdens of leadership, burdens that he did not know how to help her bear. It was she whom the Lord had chosen, and she could not let slip the mantle — even now, when she was tired to the soul.

Rendered mute by the enormity of his emotions, he again felt unmanned by her authority. Yet he did not want to question the will of the Lord God...so he did not. Forcing his questions down into his deepest heart, he ached in stricken silence for the grief they could not share.

The messenger paused at the crest of the hill, drawing his palm across his sweaty forehead. He looked at the cluster of mud-brick huts and dark-colored tents scattered haphazardly in the valley below him. The shadows cast by the sun, sinking behind the surrounding hills, made a stark patchwork of light and shadow. He had walked north for two days in the summer heat to reach Kedesh in Naphtali. Wiping his hand on the back of his leg, he started down the slope to the village.

At the well in the center of the hamlet he found a man with his servant, drawing water in a skin bucket.

"You are Barak, son of Abinoam?" the messenger said.

The stocky Naphtalite straightened slowly, his hand straying toward his belt knife as his eyes quickly skittered around the horizon. "Who wishes to know?"

"I am come from Deborah, judge of all Israel, servant of the Most High. She would speak with you."

"Surely even Jabin knows the name of Deborah," said Barak in a low voice. "What assurance have I that you lead me to her, and not to him?" His eyes still roamed the landscape for any sign of ambush.

"Deborah says this: 'The voice of Him who called to

Moses from the midst of the burning bush has spoken to me, and He now calls unto you, Barak Bar-Abinoam.' "

Barak considered for a moment, then slowly extended his arms to the sides at waist height, palms downward, and made a patting motion. At this signal, the servant at his side visibly relaxed, and the messenger allowed himself to draw a deep breath and look about.

"Where are your men concealed?" he asked. "I see no one here but us."

"That does not concern you," snapped Barak. "I will go with you." He turned to his servant: "Go to my father and tell him of this summons." The servant walked away, and Barak turned again to the messenger. "Give me a moment to gather some provisions, and we will go. I prefer to travel at night."

Barak squatted on his heels and stared dumbly at the ground between his feet. "Let me understand you," he began slowly. "You are telling me to raise ten thousand men from Zebulun and Naphtali, assemble them at Tabor, and await Sisera's pleasure?" He glared darkly up at Deborah, who sat with her back against the palm tree. Her face was now to him an unreadable tablet of stone.

He continued: "What you suggest is folly. Even with a host that size, Sisera's war chariots will cut through us like cattle. We have not the proper weapons for pitched battle on the plain. He can outflank us, rain arrows upon our heads, cut us to shreds at his whim. We can muster barely a thousand proper swords among us — and you tell me to go down to Jezreel and face Sisera?"

Barak arose, and stalked angrily back and forth. His

glance fell upon Lapidoth, who sat outside the doorway of the tent, eyes downcast.

"You!" Barak said to him. "Old man! Would you take this advice from your own wife? Would you go down and face nine hundred iron chariots with a band of stick-wielding goatherds?"

Deborah's unknowable stare creased into concern as she beheld her husband. Lapidoth looked across at her, then into Barak's angry face, then again lowered his gaze to the ground. "If the Lord so commands," he said.

Barak snorted in disgust and turned his back on them both.

As Deborah stood, righteous indignation covered her features. She paced with measured steps to Barak, stopping less than an arm's length from his back. In a controlled yet powerful voice she now spoke not as a judge, but as a prophetess, a calling she was given even before becoming Israel's leader.

"You misunderstand, son of Abinoam. I did not give you advice. What I gave you was a word from *Adonai Elohim*, the God who brought Israel up out of Egypt and caused them to cross the sea on dry ground; He who brought the people of Canaan to the edge of Joshua's sword; He who caused mighty Cushan the Doubly Wicked to fall before Othniel; He who delivered up Eglon the Moabite to be killed by Ehud the Left-Handed; He who raised up Shamgar to slay thirty score of Philistines with no weapon in his hand save a stick.

"Have you enjoyed the last twenty years, Naphtalite?" she grated. "Has it been to your liking, skulking in the hills with your rabble, making your little raids upon Jabin's cities? Does it gratify you to watch him punish your plain-dwelling brethren for your midnight bravery, bleeding them dry to fodder his war steeds?

"Now comes a chance for you to strike a telling blow, your arm strengthened by Yahweh Himself — but you prefer your own tactics. Has your strategy been so successful that you scorn the counsel of the Almighty? Perhaps you have forgotten the sins of Israel, the iniquities which caused the Lord to turn His face from us, to sell us into bondage to Jabin. For twenty long years have the cries of Jacob's children gone up before the Lord of Hosts, begging Him to again look upon us with favor, and take His scourge from us.

"His hand is upon me, Barak. His finger has touched me, and I, a poor woman of Ephraim, have been laden too long with the distress of our people. Now, Barak of Naphtali, I say to you that the Lord has called you to rise up and cast Jabin's foot off the necks of your brothers.

"You do not reject me, Barak. Know in truth that it is not merely the counsel of an old woman upon which you turn your back. No, you set your face against Him Who Is, for it is He who calls you, not I."

Deborah turned, closed her eyes, and sighed. Then the only sound was the dry whisper of the wind through the palm leaves. Slowly, Barak's shoulders sagged. For a moment his head dropped in defeat upon his chest; then, with great effort, he looked up to speak.

"Your words fall upon my ears like fire from heaven. I have fought the slow defeat in the hills, and I am bone-weary of the endless battles. But I do not wish to take the Almighty One as adversary. I will do as you — as the Lord God says.

Still, I do not have the clear vision you possess; I cannot feel His hand.

"I will go and raise the host. But...I beg you, Deborah: You must come north to Tabor. I fear that without you, the Lord's favor will not rest upon me."

Lapidoth watched Deborah as she stood silently, her eyes closing again. His frustration and incomprehension were boiling over into a torrent he could not contain.

"No! No!" he said, vaulting from his place beside the tent and moving toward the judge and the commander. "Is it not enough that she has judged these twenty years — that she makes Israel's decisions, and carries Israel's afflictions within her own soul? Would you now make her a warrior as well? I cannot have it. I cannot have her stolen from me this way."

Deborah, her expression a shifting amalgam of impatience, fear, pity, and love, regarded the raw ache etched upon her husband's face. The open sore in his heart could not be ignored. Yet she was unsure how to mitigate his confused pain, an uncertainty intensified by her not yet knowing the right response to Barak's request.

Barak looked tacitly from Deborah to Lapidoth, then quietly moved away as the old man and his wife searched each other's eyes.

Deborah did not wish to gratuitously tread upon Lapidoth's self-worth and his love for her, yet she could not allow him to set himself between her and the will of the Lord, whatever it was. "My husband," she began, moving beside him. "You must try to understand." She laid her hand gently upon his arm, but he remained tightly coiled about his pain, his wounded eyes never leaving hers, his lips pressed whitely together. "The Lord is the One who has carried events to this very juncture," she said, both to herself and to her husband. "For His glory the Lord has brought us to this very moment. I am only His instrument, that the glory of His might can be revealed. I can do nothing other than His bidding.

"Beloved, His will drives no wedge between us." She offered her hands, and he clasped them. "Surely" she went on, "it is only our failures that give birth to this bitter fear."

She paused, closing her eyes again for perhaps ten heartbeats. When she opened them and continued speaking, her voice was still calm, but firmer. "I love you as my own soul, Lapidoth. But I must see the end. The Lord has shown me this, and He will not be thwarted. I will tread His path though it cost me my life." She gazed with love and determination into her husband's eyes. They stood thus for a moment, an eternity. Then Lapidoth silently released her hands, stepped back, and walked silently away.

Deborah momentarily put a hand to her eyes, drew a deep, shuddering breath, then turned and went toward the path where Barak stood waiting.

Barak spoke first. "It is hard for your husband to see you doing...doing a man's work."

"Yes," Deborah answered with a sharpness that surprised him. She gazed beyond him, to the north — toward Zaanaim and the tents of Heber the Kenite — as she continued: "And you, Barak of Naphtali, will find it just as hard, for in the Lord's victory over Sisera, a woman — and not you — will strike the mightiest blow."

Her words were beyond him; Barak could say nothing in response.

She faced him again: "I will go with you, son of Abinoam. Prepare for the march."

Barak nodded, and she watched him walk away.

As she turned toward her tent, she saw Lapidoth approaching, carrying a sword at his side. He came and stood before her, looking down into her eyes for a long moment... then held out to her the sword.

Jabin sat in the breezy courtyard of his palace in Hazor, fastidiously licking the juice of a pomegranate from each fingertip. He asked the kneeling messenger, "Has Sisera been notified of the movement of the Hebrew forces?"

"Yes, my king. Even now Lord Sisera assembles his troops on the plain of Jezreel and stands ready to engage the enemy."

"Very well." Absorbed in thought, Jabin sucked on a bit of rind. "I suspect those Hebrew bumpkins have the notion that this unseen god of theirs will somehow carry the day. A taste of steel should cure them of their self-righteous superstitions. Tell Sisera that I most particularly want their commander — whoever he is — captured alive and brought to me here."

The king stood, tossing the pits among the flagstones, and dismissed the runner with a curt wag of his fingers. Rising, he walked to the colonnade rimming the courtyard, clasped his hands behind him, and watched the purple evening shadows steal down across the plain toward the placid surface of Lake Huleh to the east.

Sisera strode out of his pavilion, stretching and yawning in the early morning air. As he had done for several days now, he cast his eyes first to the east, to the slopes of Mount Tabor, to observe the disposition of the Hebrew army. "No change there," he mused. "Still they roost on their hillside and wait for...something. They will not come down to fight on level ground, and I will not go up to them. So, we'll watch each other a bit longer."

The next thing the general noticed was the dusty, metallic smell of rain in the air. Odd, that. A breeze had risen from the southwest, and clouds piled up in the south, from Mount Gilboa to the plain of Sharon, like banks of dirty fleece, low to the ground. In the summer one usually did not see much wet weather.

Sisera walked across the dry creek bed of the Kishon and motioned to his quartermaster. "Place an extra guard on the horses," he ordered. "If we should get a storm, they may bolt. And tell the men to stand ready to harness the chariots. I have a feeling about this day," he muttered, as the quartermaster left to carry out the orders.

Sisera, stroking his oiled and braided beard, squinted again up at Tabor, counting the columns of wispy smoke rising from the Hebrew campfires. Again he estimated the size of the force, mentally increasing his tally by a third, as was his habit. In this way he had, in the past, avoided many unpleasant surprises in the field.

He felt confident. Mobility was all, and his was the superior mobility. He sniffed and rubbed his stomach as he went back across the creek bed to his pavilion, satisfied with his preparations.

By mid-morning, under an overcast sky, the game board was set. Sisera's chariots had drawn up in long lines, one

behind the other, the triple-hitched horses tossing their manes
and whinnying nervously in the breeze. Harness chains
clinked at random as the drivers held the capering animals
sternly in check. The battle-bred steeds could smell the
coming conflict, and their hooves would not be still. Archers
checked their gear a final time as they stood beside the
drivers, tensely fingering bowstrings and securing quivers.
From the axles of each chariot protruded cruelly curved, keen
blades, honed to a razor's-edge, capable of mangling flesh
and snapping bone as they rotated with the spinning wheels.

Behind the chariot ranks deployed four phalanxes of
infantry, each warrior armed with spear, sword, and a heavy
bullhide shield. After the chariots had sufficiently weakened
the enemy, they would move in and begin the methodical
business of exterminating the remainder of the Hebrews in
hand-to-hand combat.

Sisera felt the familiar tightness in his stomach that
presaged imminent battle. He looked over the deployment of
his forces and nodded. All ready. The Hebrews, though
superior in number, would be outmaneuvered and slaughtered to the man as soon as they left their hillside. He would
take their commander, bound and gagged, to Jabin's welcom-
ing party at Hazor.

On the lower slopes of Mount Tabor, the Hebrews assembled in ragtag ranks as they awaited the word to attack. Barak
viewed his motley army and felt himself dying anew with
despair. They looked so pathetic: a scant handful had swords;
the rest were armed with mattocks, pitchforks, sickles, axes,
and whatever they had scavenged. Given Jabin's monopoly
on the smelting of iron, the Naphtalite marveled that any of

them had metal weapons. Were it not for their nighttime raids, even his own personal band would not have sword or buckler. How could they possibly hope to prevail?

Deborah climbed onto a large stone at the front of the host and raised her arms to the gray sky. "Men of Zebulun and Naphtali!" she intoned in a ringing voice. "Today shall the Lord do a great work before your eyes! You shall see His might, before which the chariots and horses of Jabin are as straw in the wind! The arm of the Lord will fight for you, and in His strength shall you lay waste the host of Sisera! Now watch and see the hand of the Almighty!"

A low rumble began in the hills to the south. On the plain, the horses neighed and tossed their heads, dancing skittishly in their harnesses. Sisera at first took the sound for distant thunder, but instead of rumbling away and diminishing, the deep reverberation sustained and grew stronger. A cold blast of air from the storm clouds caused the general to gasp and the high-strung team drawing his chariot to rear, their eyes showing white.

The sound grew louder as the drivers struggled to control the frightened beasts. The men looked all around and at each other, but none could discern the cause for this alarm.

Suddenly a wall of reddish-brown, frothy water roared out of the hills south of the plain and cascaded down the bed of the Kishon toward the astonished Hittite and his invincible army. Pandemonium erupted. Discipline instantly evaporated as each panic-stricken charioteer, unable to face what he could not fight, tried to wheel his team and race away from the water juggernaut. Axle blades slashed fetlocks and tendons of fear-crazed horses as they reared and bucked, screaming with pain and terror. Harnesses were smashed to useless fragments; drivers cursed and prayed to their several deities, vainly struggling to control their teams and escape.

The pulverizing torrent smashed into the ranks closest to the channel of the Kishon, crushing or drowning every living thing in its path. For those farther away, the situation quickly became as hopeless. The flood waters rapidly spread out over the plain, miring the wheels of the heavy war chariots in a sea of mud.

A great shout erupted from the throats of the Hebrew army, which surged down from the side of the mountain and across the plain, ready to complete the task God had begun. Unhampered by heavy armor and berserk animals, they clamored among the Canaanite army, stabbing, slashing and bludgeoning. The demoralized host of Sisera the Hittite abandoned all pretense of resistance and fled, each man intent upon saving himself. The Hebrews pursued, and slaughtered all the way from Tabor to Harosheth.

Sisera limped up the ridge, gasping for breath in the predawn darkness. He had managed to get out of his chariot before the flash flood swamped it, escaping the mayhem that befell his men. He fled north through the rugged hills of Zebulun for the better part of a day and night, provisionless. He kept below the crests of the hills, traveling in the rocky ravines whenever possible. That he was being trailed he never doubted. He must win through to Hazor, and soon, for his strength ebbed rapidly. Leaning against a boulder, he panted for breath — then straightened, wincing, and doggedly resumed his desperate journey.

Picking their way down the eastern face of the flinty slope, Barak and two servants carefully studied the ground at their feet. To eyes practiced at tracking errant sheep through stony country, signs revealed that their prey had passed this way.

"He cannot get aid in any of the villages of Zebulun or Naphtali," reasoned Barak. "By the northeastward bearing of the trail, he must be trying for Hazor. He means to take refuge behind the walls of Jabin's city. He will perhaps find it harder to enter than he anticipated."

Cautiously, Sisera peered over the edge of the gully and studied the situation below him. He was on a knoll overlooking Hazor. Between him and safety waited a company of Hebrews, encamped outside the locked city gate, newly armed with the spoils of the debacle on the Jezreel plain. Another group patrolled the perimeter in several parties of four. Clearly, no one entered or departed Hazor.

Sisera cursed the names of all the gods to whom he had lately prayed. The Hebrews clearly meant to consolidate their uncanny victory by subduing Hazor. This group was doubtless the vanguard of those who would soon besiege the city. Precious little could Jabin do about that, having committed all but a pittance of his troops to the battle on the plain.

Sisera's mind whirled. Where would he go now? His pursuers could not be more than a half-day behind. He had not slept for a day and a night. His stomach knotted like a fist from lack of food, and his throat burned with thirst.

Then he remembered: In the country up by Kedesh lived a

herdsman, Heber by name, who had dutifully paid tribute to Jabin and maintained good relations with the king. He had not taken part in the Hebrew uprising. Perhaps Sisera could rest in the tents of the Kenite long enough to regain his strength. The bedraggled general levered himself unsteadily to his feet and turned his face north, to Zaananaim, the camp of Heber.

Jael saw the staggering, tattered figure approaching as she sat at the door of her tent in the mid-afternoon heat. The camp was pitched in a small oak grove beside a spring of pure, cool water at the edge of a plain west of Kedesh. Jael's heart raced within her, for she somehow knew that with the arrival of this wounded stranger her moment of destiny had come.

"Come, my lord," she said, rising to greet the woebegone wretch limping into the grove. "Sit here in the shade."

"Water?" the stranger asked in a croaking voice. Jael rose and filled a stoneware urn from the spring. She brought it to the man, who sucked at its contents.

"Please, to whom have I the honor of offering hospitality?" the young wife inquired, knowing the answer.

The stranger stopped drinking, wiping his mouth with the back of his hand as he looked warily at her. "Whose camp is this?" he asked.

"This is the household of Heber the Kenite, my lord. And I am Jael, his wife."

The stranger heaved a sigh of relief. "I am Sisera, general of the host of Jabin, king of Hazor. I beg your mercy upon me, good wife of Heber, for the sake of the friendship between your husband and my master." The Hittite again raised the urn to his lips and drank, but his eyes never left hers.

"Your presence honors this house, Lord Sisera," replied Jael, demurely avoiding his gaze. "You are hurt, and weary beyond weariness. Come inside my tent, and rest. I will bring you food. I am alone, for my husband is in the field with the flocks, and no one is here save myself and my maidservants. Surely you have nothing to fear."

The general considered a moment. His pursuers could overtake him while he tarried here. Still, his body cried out for respite from the torture endured these last two days.

"I am grateful for your offer, woman. I will rest for a few moments, and no more. If anyone asks you, say that I passed by here, and did not stop."

"As you say, my lord."

Sisera went inside the richly furnished tent. A slight breeze blew from the south, the door arranged so that the light wind wafted inside, cooling the dark interior of the dwelling. Soft piles of sheepskins lined the walls, and Sisera chose the nearest and collapsed upon it.

Jael entered, carrying a wooden bowl filled with curds. "My lord Sisera, please accept this poor offering."

As the general took the food from her hand, he appreciatively eyed the face, neck, and arms of this generous young woman. *Heber is too old to have such beauty wasted on him,* he thought. The Hittite resolved to remember Jael when he was in more favorable circumstances.

No sooner had he eaten the curds than fatigue finally overcame him. Against the urging of his judgment, his body succumbed to the leaden shackles of exhaustion and he fell into a heavy sleep.

For a long moment, Jael studied the general's sleeping

form. Her mind raced back to the words of Deborah: "When the Lord God needs you, He will find you..." Her pulse hammered in her temples as she remembered scenes from her girlhood, before her father betrothed her to Heber. She remembered her younger brother, so strong, so vigorous, so confident. She recalled her mother's warnings to him — how she begged and pleaded with him not to go out with the Naphtalite band on their night raids. She heard again Baruch's blithe dismissal of his mother's concerns. "Jabin is a tyrant, Mother," he would say. "We must never surrender to him."

Shuddering, Jael heard again the naked screams of grief with which her mother greeted the news of her son's execution by Jabin. Her only son, now gone forever. Burned into Jael's memory for all time was the image of Baruch's flayed body, hung on the outside of the walls of Hazor, picked apart by carrion birds.

Her breath coming in gasps, Jael quietly went outside. She looked about, spied a tent nail lying nearby, its point ground to sharpness from repeated hammering into gravely soil. Finding a heavy mallet on her husband's workbench, she crept back into her tent.

Sisera, still in the narcotic embrace of slumber, lay on his back with his arms thrown wide. His breath was slow and even, his face turned toward the tent entrance. Jael approached him, staring with the intensity of a stalking predator at the visage of this man whom she feared and loathed.

She knelt beside him, placing the point of the nail, almost tenderly, upon his temple. In her heightened awareness, she was conscious of minute details: the tiny white dimple created by the tip of the spike as it pressed against his skin; the soft breath of the breeze against her cheek, the pungent smell of the sheepskins. Then she lifted the heavy mallet above his head...

Barak and his servants entered the oak grove just as Jael, her hands and forearms covered with the blood of Sisera, came out of her tent. Knowingly she looked at the Naphtalite.

"You search for Sisera the Hittite." Her tone admitted no doubt of her assumption. "Enter and see the man you seek." She pulled back the tent flap and motioned them inside.

The once mighty general of the host of Hazor lay with the tent nail jutted outward from the side of his head. The wool pallet under his head was dyed scarlet with his life's blood. His eyes, open in death, stared blindly at them as they stood wordlessly in the doorway.

Heber the Kenite, coming in from the fields, rushed in among them. "What is the meaning of this? Jael, who are these men?"

As his eyes fell upon the body of Sisera, he was struck dumb by the apparition of horror that lay upon his bed.

"Is this not Sisera, the general of Jabin's army?" His eyes were drawn helplessly to those of his wife. Jael stood silently with her shoulders back, her hands clasped before her, and her face bright with triumph.

"Have you done this thing, my wife? How... What..." Heber looked to Barak, whose face only mirrored his own incomprehension. Still silent, Barak stepped numbly outside the tent.

A woman had slain the mighty Sisera. A universe longed

for answers, but the words to frame the questions would not come.

The Hebrews came from far and wide to celebrate the victory God had given them. A great feast was spread at Chesulloth, at the feet of Mount Tabor. There they sacrificed to the Lord of Hosts, singing songs of praise and thanking Him for His great deliverance. Deborah and Barak recounted the wonders of God's miraculous salvation of His people, leading Israel in a song of joy.

> *O LORD, when you went out from Seir,*
> *when you marched from the land of Edom,*
> *the earth shook, the heavens poured,*
> *the clouds poured down water.*
> *The mountains quaked before the LORD,*
> *the One of Sinai,*
> *before the LORD, the God of Israel...*

> *Wake up, wake up, Deborah!*
> *Wake up, wake up, break out in song!*
> *Arise, O Barak!*
> *Take captive your captives, O son of Abinoam...*

> *From the heavens the stars fought,*
> *from their courses they fought against Sisera.*
> *The river Kishon swept them away,*
> *the age-old river, the river Kishon.*
> *March on, my soul; be strong!*

Most blessed of women be Jael,
   the wife of Heber the Kenite,
   most blessed of tent-dwelling women…
Her hand reached for the tent peg,
   her right hand for the workman's hammer.
She struck Sisera, she crushed his head,
   she shattered and pierced his temple.
At her feet he sank…
   where he sank, there he fell — dead.

So may all your enemies perish, O LORD!
   But may they who love you be like the sun
   when it rises in its strength.

Late that night, after a day and evening of merrymaking, Deborah and Lapidoth were finally alone in the flickering lamplight of their tent. They were joyfully reliving the celebration, fending off the tiredness they knew would soon overcome them.

"My husband," Deborah said in sudden seriousness, staring into the lamp. "Perhaps my time as judge is finished. Perhaps I've completed the Lord's work for me."

Lapidoth matched her tone in his reply: "Is this the question to weigh in His moment of victory?"

"I've thought much on it today," she said, "and have presented it to the Lord in many silent prayers. But I have no answer."

They were quiet for a while, and in the stillness they began to feel fully their weariness.

"Surely," Lapidoth said slowly, "you have been faithful in

the work for which God has raised you up. Only He can tell
you if that work is now completed. And tell you He will.

"But," he added with a smile, "perhaps not tonight."

Deborah returned his smile, and folded his hands in hers.
"Then in this, His moment of victory, I will indeed celebrate
what the Lord has done. I can do nothing but His bidding."

A JAGGED ARC of lightning bolted across the turbid night sky, momentarily freezing everything in a blue flash of incandescence. A concussion of thunder shook the ground with a chest-pounding blast, like boulders being ripped apart by giants. Wind-whipped rain lashed across the Arnon River, pelting the three mud-and-wattle huts in the scrub oak grove with stinging pebbles of moisture.

The goats penned near the huts panicked. Surging against the sapling which served as a gate, they toppled it and raced pell-mell into the darkness with loud bleats of alarm.

Kilion, lying on his bed inside the hut nearest the pens, heard the commotion made by the frightened livestock. He arose, cursing the stupidity of all animals. "Orpah, the flock has stampeded — I'll have to go and regather them, before they run all the way to the Red Sea. I'll return by morning."

As he spoke, he threw on a robe, grabbed a hide to fend off

the rain, and took his staff in his hand. He ducked through the
low doorway into the storm, meeting Mahlon, his younger
brother, who next door had also been awakened by the noise.

Orpah heard her husband and his brother shouting at
each other as they ran off into the downpour to find their
animals. For a long while she lay awake, flinching at each
loud burst of thunder, listening to the moaning of the wind
through the oak branches. Eventually the lightning and
thunder subsided into a quiet, steady drizzle, and she fell
back into sleep.

In the morning, with the night's rain puddled in the
doorway of the hut and dripping through gaps in the wattle,
Orpah awoke alone. She felt — not for the first time — a
longing for her father's house in Ar. Made of sturdy clay brick,
it did not leak like this poor mud hut. There, she had not been
forced to endure the smell of goat dung. And the religious
customs of her own people had been a comfort, unlike the
austere devotion to an invisible, nameless god practiced by
her husband, his brother and mother. She felt alone here, and
not just because Kilion was gone from their bed.

Orpah peered out her doorway. The morning was crys-
talline, the early sunlight captured by each wet blade of grass
as it filtered through the trees. She left her hut in the grove and
climbed the flinty cutbank of the Arnon. Shading her eyes, she
stared east into the sunrise, looking along the river for some
sign of her husband's return. As she turned west, she noticed
her sister-in-law, perched on a rock some paces from her
position, also searching the terrain. She clambered over the
rocky, sloping ground to Ruth.

"Have you seen them?" Orpah asked.

"No. But I don't think the goats would climb out of the valley, do you? Surely the men will be able to gather them in the low places and drive them back here."

Orpah nodded. Perhaps. She did not care about the fate of goats, but she knew Kilion would not rest until they were safely back in the fold. Sometimes she was certain he cared more for his husbandry of the livestock than for her.

She observed Ruth, studying the vista to the west. Like herself, Ruth was of Moab, born and raised in Ar. Her hair was auburn, unlike that of most girls in the region, whose tresses tended to be dark brown or black. Ruth appeared simple and open — attractive more for the purity and innocence of her countenance than for any classic proportions or features. Her family, as Orpah recalled, were not among the wealthy in Ar. And, unlike herself, Ruth seemed quite content to be the wife of a Hebrew goatherd.

Orpah sighed. "I'm hungry. I'm going down now. Are you coming?"

"No, I'll stay here and watch a little longer."

Orpah turned to go.

"Orpah?"

She paused, looking over her shoulder at the younger woman. "Yes?"

"Orpah...you don't think...you don't think they could have been hurt, do you?" A childish fear shone from Ruth's eyes, pleading for comfort, for reassurance. Until now, it had not occurred to Orpah to worry about Kilion or Mahlon.

"No. No, I'm sure they'll be back soon. Don't fret." Orpah climbed down toward the homestead while Ruth resumed her vigil.

At mid-afternoon the two young women were weeding the soggy grainfield by the river. Augmented by the previous night's rainfall, the river flowed swiftly, heavy and brown with soil washed from the hills on both sides. As the women worked, they heard the bleating of the goats. At the first faint sound of the returning flock, Ruth dropped her mattock and raced out to meet them. She saw Kilion, wearily driving before him the small herd of frightened animals — and over his shoulder was slung a dark figure, wet and lifeless. Ruth recognized immediately the body of Mahlon.

Ruth's grief was leaden, her despair alleviated only by the gentle glimmer of courage in the eyes of her mother-in-law, who met them at the door of her hut.

Naomi reached toward her youngest son as his body was laid on a pallet. Kilion sank nearby. His face was ashen, fatigue and sorrow written in his eyes.

Ruth and Naomi kneeled before the pallet. Naomi's hand paused as she stroked the cold brow of Mahlon. She glanced up at Kilion, whose body was now shaking with a deep, rattling cough.

Orpah held him tightly. She spoke with a trembling voice: "I…I am afraid, Mother." Naomi rose, and Orpah felt the old woman's hand rest briefly on her shoulder, and heard the creaking of her bones as she left again to comfort Ruth.

That evening the ague fastened Kilion in a red-hot grip. Before Orpah's eyes, it sucked the life from his body, even as she applied every poultice, herb, and other treatment she knew of.

The prospect of his death unnerved her. The future without him was a thought too unbearable to entertain. But the terrible unknown was not to be denied. Sickness was eating away the frail cord binding Kilion's spirit within his flesh.

In the darkness after midnight, by the shuddering light of a tallow lamp, Orpah watched as Kilion drew his final, quivering breath. His eyes snapped open and glazed, and his chest dropped in a slow sigh as passive as the falling of a leaf.

Orpah felt the pent-up tide of fear bursting from her in a black wail of agony, as she squatted in the center of the dark hut, the dark night, the dark world. Unable and unwilling to abate the harsh catharsis, she covered her face in her arms and let the acrid flood pour from her.

Only days later, three women stood on the hillside above the cutbank. Two new cairns marked the graves of the brothers. Three women shared the unwelcomed communion of grief as old as Eve.

That night, as Naomi mourned the loss of her sons in voluntary solitude, Orpah shared her hut with Ruth, discussing their bleak future.

"I will stay with Naomi," announced Ruth, her voice cracking with emotion. "I shall not go back to Ar. I cannot go back to my father's house."

"Did your father treat you cruelly?"

"Oh no, not that. It's just...that my father isn't a wealthy man—"

Embarrassed by Ruth's candor, Orpah remained silent.

"I once heard my father talking to some of the priests of

Astarte...about me," Ruth continued. "If Mahlon hadn't visited our village when he did, I think my father would have sold me to the temple."

"Worse fates could come to a woman than to serve the goddess," Orpah responded. "At least you would have been well fed, perhaps even respected."

"Hah! Respect? I've heard the men snicker when they talk about the priestesses. They have something else on their minds when they go there, no matter how much fuss and to-do is made. And have you never seen what happens when a woman becomes too old to be useful?"

"No — I suppose I hadn't thought about it..."

"No one thinks about it, and no one cares when a worn-out priestess is sold to the beggars for a few small coins in the temple coffers. Because there are more girls where she came from. So I will stay with Naomi and I will serve her god. And when I am old, perhaps I will possess her faith and strength."

Orpah was surprised by the vehemence in Ruth's voice, and angered by her out-of-hand rejection of the gods of their people. "What good has Naomi's god done for us?" she demanded. "Look at us! We live in huts that barely keep out the rain, our husbands have been ripped from our breasts by chasing a few miserable goats through a storm, and we are left childless, destitute! I prefer gods I can see and handle. This blind trust of Naomi's is a chasing after wind. Her mumbled prayers and mute acceptance of catastrophe don't make sense!

"Her god is a mountain of sand; you can't get to the top and you can't dig to the bottom. So why try? Why waste your life on a god like that? If you choose to do so, your fate will be

what you deserve! As for myself, I have a home in Ar, and I
will go back to it."

In the morning, Naomi gathered her daughters-in-law and
told them of her intention to return to the homeland of her
youth, Israel. "Moab has devoured my husband and my sons,"
she said. "I cannot stay here. You both should also return to
your own people. You are young; you can begin again." As
the old woman smiled sadly at her, Orpah felt embarrassed by
the doubts she harbored about Naomi and her god.

"Mother," she said, "you cannot go alone. We will go
with you—"

"No, child," interrupted the old woman. "Your place is
not in Israel. You must marry again in the land of your mother
and father. I will ask the Almighty to help you, to send you
another husband to comfort you in your loss."

Orpah, hearing her own desire commingled with the will
of Naomi's god, could not protest further. She did not wish to
be unkind to this woman who had loved her as a daughter —
yet she could not take comfort in some notion that the
nameless one cared about her circumstances.

She nodded. Breaking into tears, she fell into Naomi's
arms. A long time passed while they stood clasped in each
other's embrace. Orpah slowly relaxed, and for several
moments looked intently into the worn, sad face of the older
woman. Nodding once more in sorrow, she turned to her own
tent to begin packing her few possessions.

Naomi turned to Ruth, who stood with tears streaming
down her cheeks. A determined line was carved into the set of
her jaw. "Mother, do not ask me to leave you, for I cannot. I

will stay with you, and make my home with you. I will take your people as my own, and worship your god. I will live and die in your land, and my bones shall rest there. May your god punish me with the worst of fates if I ever leave your side."

Her bright eyes penetrated Naomi's melancholy, convincing her the choice was final. The faintest wisp of joy brushed Naomi's lips as she stroked the girl's copper tresses.

The next day at sunset the three women embraced for the last time. Their shared sorrow melted into a common flow of tears. Reasoning that unaccompanied women travel safest at night, they parted, Orpah turning south, Ruth and Naomi fording the Arnon and striking northward.

Naomi turned to look one last time upon the small grove of scrub oaks. Then she turned, slipping her arm through Ruth's, and began the long journey home. Six days would bring the old widow and her daughter-in-law round the Salt Sea and into Judah.

After a night of walking, Ruth and Naomi lay down in the shelter of a rock overhang, waiting out the heat of the day. The sun burned in a brassy sky, pulling translucent waves of warmth from the ground.

While Naomi slept, Ruth kept watch. With the head of her mother-in-law in her lap, she leaned against the cool, shaded stone, feeling Naomi's shoulders rise and fall with each breath. Ruth saw weathered beauty in the old woman's features; the kind of beauty she recognized in ancient trees or hills sculpted by time — durable beauty.

Ruth drew on Naomi's stamina through the wilderness of Moab. From time to time she had noticed the older widow's lips mouthing a silent prayer to her God, her Most High. When Ruth believed her mother-in-law's strength nearly gone, Naomi kept on, breathing in new vigor from reserves of faith and hope stored up in years long past.

Ruth wondered. She had always prayed to the Baals, had carried their totems and rubbed them for luck. Her people prayed to Astarte for the assurance of abundant crops and herds. They sacrificed their own children to appease Chemosh and avert disasters. But it always seemed that her people viewed the gods as creatures like themselves — capricious forces to be feared, appeased, manipulated.

Naomi appeared to have no such view of her God. In fact, she seemed to have little understanding of Him at all. To her, He was unknowable, invisible, utterly impenetrable. Though Naomi carried no likeness of Him, no charm or talisman to invoke Him, she spoke as if He was ever near. And she ascribed to Him all power. There seemed to be no circumstance beyond His reach, no event in which His hand could not be traced. If Naomi prospered, it was because of His mercy. If she perished, she was still under His mercy. It appeared strange to Ruth that Naomi viewed both eventualities as equal manifestations of God's presence.

In Ruth's homeland, if a man's flocks fell to disease or his children became ill, it was assumed he had attracted the unfavorable attentions of some god or demon. He would consult the priests and offer a sacrifice to the offended deity. Misfortune was punishment to be averted as much as possible, not a condition to be accepted as God's will.

Here was a woman whose life was marred by tragedy. Was she seeking a new patron deity or offering sacrifices to appease a maleficent baal? In her prayers to her invisible Most High, she did not rail against the misery of her life, but asked for strength to bear the pain placed upon her.

Naomi awoke, blinking, looking up at Ruth.

"You have rested well, Mother?"

"Yes, daughter," Naomi answered, rising. "Now you must try to sleep. It cannot be more than a single watch until sundown, and then we must be on our way." Naomi reached into her bundle, pulling a piece of dried goat's meat off the dwindling haunch that must sustain them until they reached Bethlehem. "I will eat now, and watch. Rest, my child."

Ruth settled against the cool stone and closed her eyes. Just before sleep took her, she wondered if Naomi's God would ever speak to her.

The two travelers reached Naomi's hometown of Bethlehem at mid-morning of the sixth day. A party drawing water at the village well saw them struggling wearily up the trail. Shading their eyes against the sun's glare, the village women took in the approaching figures.

"Naomi?" one of them said. "Is that Naomi, wife of Elimelech, returning alone?" Together they studied the figures more closely.

"Naomi! It is Naomi!" They hurried down the trail to embrace her, exclaiming over her return.

"Sisters," she said when they had quieted, "do not call me Naomi, for I cannot be cheerful. The Lord has made my lot harsh. He has taken away my husband and my sons, and I have none to comfort me, save this, my son's widow, Ruth of

Moab. No, you must no longer call me Naomi. My name shall be *Marah,* for the Lord has dealt bitterly with me."

Accompanying Naomi and Ruth to the house of Geshur, cousin of Elimelech, the villagers wept to hear Naomi's story.

Geshur welcomed them and said, "Naomi, wife of my cousin, the house you left ten seasons ago still stands empty. Go and dwell there, and may the Almighty at last grant you rest from your wandering."

Boaz stepped outside in the early dawn, drinking the cool air in great draughts. He looked at the jagged pink line, rimmed by blue, atop the hills of Ammon. The day would be fair; a good sign for the beginning of barley harvest. The winter rains had been bountiful, the crop one of the best in memory. The Most High smiled upon them this year.

In the semi-darkness of the morning, the houses of Bethlehem looked like dark stone piles scattered randomly across the hills. Here and there, people stirred about quietly, gathering wood for a cooking fire or sharpening a sickle in preparation for the day's work. Boaz enjoyed the sharp scent of wood smoke mingling with the mellow, yeasty smell of the ripening grain in the fields. He looked south, across the low, rambling rock walls that terraced the hillsides. The early morning breeze rippled across the fields of barley, the whiskered heads of grain bobbing heavily on their browning stalks. He eagerly anticipated the cutting of the stalks, the metallic swish of the sickles.

Boaz would attend to his flocks, pastured among the valleys north of town, first thing this morning. He would go

and confer with his herdsmen, returning to his fields by noon
to assess the progress of the men.

The midday sun warmly caressed the back of Boaz's neck
as he climbed the hill toward the acacia tree where Eliab, his
overseer, leaned, observing the laborers. Reaching the crest,
he hailed Eliab as he wiped his brow with his forearm. Across
the field they could see the men stooping low, their sickles
rising and falling to the rhythm of harvest as they mowed the
stalks of grain and formed them into windrows. Women came
along behind, bundling mounds into sheaves, tying them up
with a practiced twist of the wrist. The sheaves stood in rows,
ready to be taken to the threshing floor.

At the end of the line of women, an unfamiliar worker
gathered loose stalks of grain missed by the harvesters.

"Eliab," Boaz asked, "whose maidservant gleans behind
the women?"

"Daughter-in-law of Naomi, your cousin's widow."

"The Moabite girl?"

"The same. She came to Bethlehem a widow in her own
right. Shortly after first light she came to me asking permission
to gather the waste grain, and has worked steadily since."

"I would like to meet this industrious young foreigner!"

Eliab left Boaz and hurried to the end of the field, spoke
briefly to Ruth, and motioned toward the tree where Boaz
waited. Ruth straightened slowly, putting her hand to the small
of her back and wincing as the strained muscles protested.
Boaz noticed Ruth look in his direction apprehensively, then
fold the corners of her cloak over the grain it held, tying a
knot to secure it.

♦

Sweat beaded Ruth's upper lip and pasted a few strands of copper-colored hair to her forehead as she approached Boaz with a hasty explanation. "Sir, I received permission from your headman before I..."

Boaz smiled at her. There was a tug at his heart as he looked into Ruth's wide, sensitive eyes. Sternly he suppressed nascent feelings of affection; had he not been widowed these twenty seasons?

"Here is what you must do," he said, interrupting the disturbing thoughts creeping into his mind. "Work behind my gleaners as long as you like. Stay with my people as they harvest in this field and the next. I will give them notice that you are to continue with them. I have warned the men not to touch you — you who are so lovely..." Boaz stopped speaking, surprising himself by the turn of this last phrase.

"...And when you get thirsty," he continued quickly, "you may drink from the water jars brought to the field."

"My lord," she cried, bowing to the ground, "your kindness is beyond what I deserve! Why should you honor me?"

"You have earned it in advance. I have heard of your devotion to Naomi, though she was not of your people or your customs. This has earned for you my esteem and gratitude." Boaz felt his tongue thickening with emotion, swollen by words begging to be unleashed. In a barely audible voice he managed to add, "Don't let me keep you from your work. Go back and gather all the grain you need."

A shy, heart-stopping smile came to Ruth's lips as she rose and went back to the field.

"Eliab, this maid may glean behind you throughout

harvest. Allow her free access to the leavings — in fact, do not forbid her even if she gathers from among the sheaves. Better still, have the women pull some of the stalks from among the sheaves and leave them for her...And what are you grinning at?" demanded Boaz suddenly.

"Nothing, my lord — nothing at all. It will be done as you say." Eliab hurried away, hiding the amused look on his face from his master.

The violet shadows of the hills stretched their fingers toward the east as Naomi and Ruth sat at the door of the house, eating roasted grain. "Surely the Lord has smiled upon us," Naomi said. "Where did you labor, my daughter, that you gathered in a full *ephah* of barley?"

"In the fields of Boaz, Mother."

"Doubly blessed be he!" exclaimed Naomi. "This man is the kinsman of Elimelech. May the Almighty credit it to him, that he had pity upon two poor women."

"Not only did he permit me to glean behind his servants, but he also asked me to stay with them until harvest is over. His graciousness amazed me, for I have less standing with him than any one of the servant girls!"

Naomi's eyes narrowed for a moment as she studied Ruth's face. The young woman squirmed under her gaze, color rising in her cheeks. The older woman nodded her head. "Yes, my daughter, it is well that you stay in the fields of Boaz. Perhaps you will find a rich harvest there. No doubt you will be well cared for." Naomi chuckled softly to herself, and arose to prepare for bed.

Boaz lay staring at the moonlit ceiling of his chamber. Though the grain harvest proceeded well into its second week, and he was happily exhausted, sleep evaded him tonight. The image of Ruth paraded before him, whether his eyes were open or closed.

Foolishness, he thought repeatedly. It was not appropriate at his age and station in life to be smitten like a colt by the face of a much younger woman. He found himself neglecting his flocks and unable to concentrate on his accounts. One lame excuse after another took him to the grain fields, though Eliab was a perfectly capable manager.

Since Milcah had died bearing a stillborn child, Boaz had never entertained the thought of granting another woman access to his heart. He had been severed from his wife and from the hope of children in one cruel stroke. The joy of anticipation had become a double blow of crushing grief.

No, love exacted too fearful a cost, exposed a person to far too much pain. Boaz opted to sublimate his yearning for a woman into his estate. His herds became the sleekest, his flocks the most productive, his fields the most fertile. The energy and passion other men poured into their families he poured into his work. If he could not leave children to the world, he would leave his reputation. Hollow comfort on a lonely night, but less hazardous.

Now came this beautiful stranger, rekindling fires he had long ago banked. He needn't journey to Moab to find a woman as graceful and good. Why was his soul captivated by her? Boaz groaned, turning over on his pallet. "Why, Sovereign Lord?" he sighed. "Why now, after all these years?

And why a Moabitess?" He begged for light, for guidance. He
begged for rest.

Summer's heat had begun to brown the verdancy of
spring across the hills of Judah. The barley harvest was
complete, and the wheat gathering nearly so. With a sigh,
Naomi admitted there would soon be nothing left for Ruth to
glean. Weeds grew in what had been Elimelech's grain field.
She could avoid it no longer: With the few pieces of silver
earned (by selling the goats) in Moab almost gone, Naomi had
no choice but to sell the land her husband had owned. What
she could realize from the transaction might be able to
provide a living for herself several years longer. But Ruth
deserved more...

When Ruth returned from her gleaning that evening,
Naomi inquired, "Did you see Boaz today, my daughter?"

"Oh, yes, Mother. He comes each day to the fields to eat
with...with the workers."

Naomi took her by the shoulders. "Ruth, your manner
gives the lie to your words. Is it not *you* our kinsman comes to
see, and not the servants of his house?"

Ruth's abashed silence was all the answer needed.

"Daughter, you must not be ashamed. Boaz is a righteous
man, and a wealthy one. He is taken with you, and unless I
miss my guess, you are not displeased with his attentions. Am
I blind, that I should not see the joy with which you greet him
in the marketplace? Should I not notice the way his eyes
follow you when we pass him on the way to the well? He is
older than you, it is true, but he is far from old."

Ruth looked intently into Naomi's eyes. The older woman

continued: "Boaz is our kinsman. Among our people, a kinsman is expected to provide heirs for a relative who dies childless. I can no longer produce offspring to carry on Elimelech's name. But you are young, and should again know the embrace of a husband.

"I believe Boaz is more than willing to take you as wife, but is afraid to initiate such an agreement. Now then, here is what you must do..."

Night settled warmly over Bethlehem. Torches surrounded the threshing floor, flickering merrily on the village men as they gathered to celebrate the harvest of a bountiful crop.

No one would go hungry in Bethlehem this year — and the excess grain could be sold or bartered to others in need. The mood was jolly as the men ate and drank, sharing the happy satisfaction of toil accomplished together.

The night wore on and the revelers, one by one, drifted into the darkness beyond the torchlight to sleep, their bellies taut with feasting, their heads fuzzy with wine. The torches sputtered and went out. Soon, only the moon lit the threshing floor, the quiet broken only by crickets and the snores of weary harvesters.

Ruth picked her way carefully among the slumbering revelers, unwilling to tread upon anyone's leg or arm. The summer air was pleasant, and the men had lain down this way and that upon the grass, sleeping just as they had fallen. Ruth carried no light, navigating the tangle of bodies only by the pale glow of the moon.

At last she found Boaz, sprawled on the ground at a slight remove from the others. His head was thrown back and he sucked great noisy gouts of air into his open mouth. Despite her nervousness, she smiled at the sight. Taking a deep breath, moving as quietly as she could, she spread her cloak on the ground at the feet of Boaz, as Naomi had advised her, and lay down upon it.

In the wee hours, the dream came to him, as it did almost every night. He was walking in a field of ripe grain, alone. Suddenly he turned, hearing a footstep behind him. Ruth stood before him, smiling gently, holding out her arms, beckoning. He turned, his feet like heavy stones. He strained to respond to her, but could not move his limbs. As though he was transformed into granite, he could not move toward her. And still she stood, smiling and beckoning. He must reach her! He must touch her, tell her...

"Ruth! Wait, Ruth! I will come — please don't leave..." He woke himself by his own dream-drunk shouting and sat bolt upright, his eyes wide with the vividness of the illusion. But unlike countless other nights, when he opened his eyes this time, Ruth was still there. He stared, expecting her to melt away into the fabric of the night. But she still sat at his feet. He could smell the musk in her hair, see the oil glisten on her smooth skin.

"Ruth! I dreamed...I saw...Why are you here?" he stammered.

The young woman swallowed dryly and said, "My lord, I have come to ask you...to ask you to take me as your wife. You are my kinsman, and it falls to you to do the levirate duty, to produce heirs for Elimelech and for Mahlon, his son."

Boaz was totally unprepared to hear his fantasy verbalized by its object. For a long moment the stars swirled about his head; he drowned in the dizziness of a thirsty man who chances upon a spring in the desert.

Ruth interpreted his silence as disapproval. "If my words displease you..."

"No, no! I am...I am far from displeased. May the Lord bless you for not desiring a younger man, be he rich or poor. Instead you have chosen to bring your noble spirit to me, though I am greater in years. You do not displease me, Ruth. You show me kindness and honor." Gently he reached out to take her hand. "Everyone in Bethlehem knows you are a woman of great character. Your honesty and your steadfast love for Naomi have endeared you to me; yet I am not your closest kinsman. Geshur must be allowed first right. If he will redeem you, he must be permitted. But if he will not, you must know already that my heart has spoken, over and over, its willingness. Stay here tonight, and in the morning the matter will be decided."

He removed his cloak and placed it about her shoulders. Then he lay down again, motioning for her to do the same. Pretending sleep, his mind sang her name like a psalm throughout the long night.

At dawn, before the other men began stirring, Boaz arose and woke Ruth. "Ruth, you must leave now. Don't let it be known that you came to the threshing floor this night. And take this to Naomi."

He filled Ruth's cloak with six double-handfuls of barley. She began to speak, but he held his finger to his lips. He smiled, and cupped her chin in his hand for a moment. Then he turned and walked away toward the village.

At mid-morning, Boaz was waiting at the city gate among the old villagers, butterflies dancing in his belly. It had come from her own lips! She wanted to be his! His heart could scarcely allow itself to believe.

It remained to be seen if Geshur would exercise his prerogative. When he finally happened along, Boaz took a deep breath.

"The Lord be with you, Geshur! Come; we have business to discuss."

Geshur hurried over to Boaz, who was leaning against a wall, trying to appear relaxed. "What is it, my cousin?"

"I wish to purchase the plot of land formerly owned by Elimelech, our clansman. Naomi wants to sell the land, and I want to buy it. But you are first in line, being of closer kin than I. I wanted to know if you are willing to redeem the land from Naomi."

"I would like to have the land," said Geshur.

Boaz shuddered inwardly, and continued: "Then you must know that with the land goes the levirate obligation to Elimelech. You must take Ruth the Moabitess to wife, and preserve the seed of our deceased cousin."

The elderly men seated about nodded sagely, studying Geshur's reaction. Geshur scratched his beard, squinting and grimacing at the ground a long time before he spoke.

"Then I cannot take the land. Taking another wife might sully the line of my heirs. I will have to let the land pass to you."

"Is this your final word?" asked Boaz, hardly daring to breathe.

"Yes, I have made up my mind," announced Geshur, decisively. The old men nodded, and winked to one another. Geshur signified the binding of the agreement in the customary way, taking off his sandal and offering it to Boaz. As Boaz took the sandal, he turned to the old men.

"You are my witnesses that I receive from Geshur the right to redeem the property of Naomi, and that I take Ruth the Moabitess as my wife."

The old men solemnly raised their hands and nodded, murmuring their acceptance of the proper forms. At last, Boaz was able to draw a free breath. He turned away, walking toward home, a grin spread across his face. The villagers watched him leave, and punched each other in the ribs, chuckling.

Ruth lay exhausted as the midwife took the child to clean the birth-blood from his face. Her fatigue overcame her joy, and she lapsed into a deep sleep. She had borne a boy-child. A son...

She awoke in a huge, mist-filled room. A shaft of brilliant light stabbed the haze, falling upon a throne; huge, white, empty. Majestically it seemed to float upon the swirling vapor. A man appeared from behind the throne, a king. Ruth looked closely at him, for his face was — her own! Even his hair had the same ruddy hue as hers. Without removing his gaze from her, he paced slowly to the front of the throne and sat down. It was plain that he knew her.

The mist cleared somewhat, and Ruth became conscious of another presence in the huge hall, standing behind the throne. She was filled with an overwhelming desire to worship, and she fell to her knees in awe. As she did so, she noticed that the king she had seen sitting on the throne was now kneeling as well.

The Presence, too, was a King. The white throne belonged to Him, but could not contain Him. The whole world could not contain Him. She raised her eyes slowly, slowly to His face, and beheld there — again, a face like her own. She was not afraid, for He knew her name.

"Ruth."

A faint echo reverberated tenuously through the corridors of her sleeping mind.

"Ruth."

A bit stronger this time, a bit more insistent.

"Ruth — wake up, beloved."

Her husband called her. She opened her eyes, smiling into his smile as Boaz leaned lovingly above her.

"My wife, the Lord has blessed us with a fine, strong son. Is it not a fine thing that He has spoken to us in this way?"

She nodded, her throat tight with emotion. *Yes. A fine thing, indeed.*

THE DOG SIDLED UP and cautiously pushed its nose toward the motionless huddle of soiled rags, skin, and bones. Catching the odor, it snorted in disgust and slinked off toward a nearby dung heap. The old woman, roused from a fitful slumber by the snuffling approach of the beast, glanced up at the sky. Evening. Time to go in out of the night wind. She painfully pulled herself upright and noticed the pitiful form of her husband, sprawled on a pile of ashes. She spat in his direction, and hobbled off.

As she limped toward the darkened house, she heard once more faint echoes of laughter and music. This place had once been the source of her happiness. She had raised children here, commanded a large staff of servants, presided over the wealth once amassed by the wretch lying yonder. She looked back over her shoulder at him, and spat again. That pitiful fool was too blind to recognize the cause of their tragedy.

It seemed like yesterday. Her handmaid was grooming her hair with an ivory comb inlaid with tiny emeralds. Fresh sea air wafted through the high-beamed halls, softly billowing the sheer draperies at her windows, and spreading the perfume of flowers through the house. She heard the laughter of the servants' children playing outside, and the cooks bustling around their morning fires, preparing for another day.

Her housemaids were late from their errands to the field-hands. At last one of them burst right into the dressing chamber with bloodied clothes and face. "The Sabeans!" exclaimed the hysterical maid. "They murdered everyone...all the servants are dead. Only I escaped. They took everyone... and every ox and donkey..."

The housemistress sought her husband immediately, finding him at the manor gate, eyes swollen with tears. His herd manager was limping toward them, shrieking with pain, his skin badly burned. "Forest fire," he cried. "In the hills... grass fire...all the flocks perished, every herdsman consumed in the flames..."

Suddenly another servant rushed upon them, dazed and terrified. "The master's camels — the entire herd — taken by Chaldean raiders! And all your servants were butchered by their swords!"

In three swift strokes the family was destitute. The foundations of her secure world crumbled swiftly beneath her.

"The children!" she had cried. "We will find comfort in our children."

Now her husband spoke. "Children? They are dead," he pronounced. "All ten...our sons, our daughters...dead. They were feasting at the home of their elder brother when a mighty wind swept in from the desert against the house. The walls collapsed, crushing them all."

Winter rushed through her veins. Slowly her knees crumpled, and she pressed her face into the ground. Her husband ripped his clothes into tatters and began to pull at the hair of his head. "Naked I came into the world," he had chanted, "and naked I shall depart. The Lord gave, and the Lord has taken away. Blessed be the name of the Lord."

At this, her head snapped up and she gasped in disbelief through a grief-rasped throat.

Her steps echoed through the house like laughter in a tomb. Everywhere vacancy mocked her, broke her with painful realization of what was lost. And why? Hadn't Job faithfully performed the prescribed religious duties? (At times she had, in fact, thought him foolish for the lavish excess of his devotions.) So why this sudden, irrevocable punishment? She doubted not for an instant its source: Loss this total could arise only from the power of a vengeful, capricious deity.

She wandered the barren dwelling, bitterness gnawing her heart: *The blame can only be placed upon Job's God.* Toward this deity there blazed in her soul a futile hatred, a voiceless wrath like a raging inferno.

They had still been in shock when Job's skin began erupting in pus-filled boils. *Will he finally see the uselessness of his piety?* wondered his wife. *What good will his prayers do now?*

She had confronted him: "Can you sink lower? God has abandoned you, cast you aside as carelessly as a child tires of a toy. He cannot hurt you any worse, even by death, for your life is a miserable mockery. Only time lies between you and the void. Welcome death, for it is the only comfort remaining. Curse him! Curse your God, and perhaps he will bless you with death! Curse him, for worshiping him has brought you where you are now."

"Shall I accept good from God and refuse trouble?" Job had replied calmly. His trusting eyes convinced her he was oblivious to the absurdity of his words.

In loathing she had turned from him, vowing to hate God to her dying day. And with her last breath she would curse Job to his face, if he still had one then.

The ragged, ravaged woman awoke in her crumbled alcove to the sound of mourning and weeping. She peeked through a hole in the wall and recognized four men, friends of Job, seated around his tortured body.

Seven days and nights the four sat weeping, bringing no comfort, no hope. Friends. Hah! Fine friends, who finally speak only to bring discourse and debate. She had no need of friends.

In spite of herself, she listened to their parley as the men began to berate Job for concealing sin and refusing to repent. She heard her husband staunchly defend his righteousness. He dared to maintain his innocence. He stubbornly declared his determination to plead his case before his God.

They are fools, she thought, *the lot of them!* Job's friends supposed that God needed a reason, an excuse to inflict misery on mankind. And Job persisted in viewing this farce in terms of guilt or innocence. The idiots could not see what was as plain as the scabs on Job's face: God requires no reason other than his own whim, takes no note of fault nor purity. He pours his bowls of woe upon the earth, splashing wicked and righteous alike with the fiery baths of perdition. From God, she expected nothing else.

The men prated on and on for days. She grew weary of their tedious chasing after some hare they'd never catch, and fell into the habit of sleeping during their useless debates. One day, as she slept, they suddenly stopped speaking. A hush, a stillness fell, as though the world waited in an immense, silent prelude.

Far out on the plain to the west, a small vortex wind spiraled wisps of dust into the air. Instead of skipping feebly along the ground and fading, the vortex intensified. It swelled into a whirling funnel sucking all the winds of heaven to its center. With the majestic inexorability of an avalanche or tidal wave, it bore down on the place where they sat. They felt it to be stalking them, measuring them. They knew.

The men were already on their faces in the dust when the Voice spoke. They knew, amid the jangling terror erupting inside them, that the roar was a Voice. But of the five, only Job seemed to be actually listening, as if hearing in a familiar language the voice of an ally.

The last echo of thunder died away among the hills, and the old woman stirred in her slumber, roused by a vague dream of an inescapable terror. She sat up, blinking, and glanced out at the men. *Still there, the fools,* she thought. She pulled her meager rags closer, and lay back down to sleep.

Fathers & Sons

WHO IS THAT MAID I see gliding through my palace courtyard? Ah...my granddaughter Tamar. Absalom's child. As beautiful as her namesake — my daughter, my own precious Tamar.

Tamar, my child... Was it so long ago I watched you strolling happily within these same walls? *O Tamar...* Would to God I had kept you safe!

O, but Tamar! How could I have known that Amnon, your own brother, would be so depraved as to force himself upon you?

And how could I know of the wounded rage Absalom was hiding — a rage for the shame perpetrated on you, his favorite sister? For I was blind. I could only look on as he sprang his terrible trap. My son the murderer, slaying my son the rapist.

What could I have done after that? I could scarcely have ignored Absalom's guilt. For five years I pretended he did not exist, though there was not a day I did not long to be with him again.

It required the subterfuge of Joab — Joab! — to bring him again into my presence. But by then, of course, it was too late. Too much bitterness. Too much rancor. I could no longer be his father — only his commander-in-chief.

I've rehearsed the grounds for his grievances against me so many times that their taste has become a constant coating on my tongue. I can't in a lifetime write enough poetry to flush that gall from my throat. Countless the times I've recalled scenes from his boyhood, times I could have taught him, tried to lead him. I do not find it within myself to blame him for what he did. Nathan's words thunder again in my mind. How should I — who for lust slew a loyal servant — decry Absalom for seeking a prize he desired? If he failed to heed, was it not for lack of example?

He was a good-looking boy. I remember him striding around my household with that confident look on his face. All the young women of Jerusalem admired him. At first I thought this was flattery directed at me, but it was soon apparent that he cultivated the effect of his own handsome visage.

He used to loiter in the barracks and listen to the lies the men told each other. He'd slap his knees, bellowing at every crude joke, then gaze raptly at the old campaigners as they rambled on about our days on the run in the desert. Little enough glamor there had been in those days, but I suppose almost anything looks different when enough time has passed. Anyway, the boy soaked it up greedily.

I had named him Absalom—"Prince of Peace" — but what folly that was! He brought little enough peace, that's certain. Born during a lull in the constant fighting of those days, perhaps his name was a fond wish that the bloodshed would stop.

I suppose Solomon will reign after me. He'll do fine; he's a clever boy. I hope he rules in peace — that his name doesn't become an obscene parody of his life. God knows his father has washed the land in enough blood for any two kings.

But it is the blood of Absalom that cries out to me every night. It drowns out all the myriad voices of the others I have slain.

O Absalom, my son, my son! Sometimes I see you hanging in the tree by your lush hair, swinging back and forth, with Joab's darts in your belly. And you open your dead eyes and look down at me and say, "You have killed me, loving father."

O, God! I told them to be careful! "Watch out for Absalom!" I said. "He's just a boy!" I said.

But he's dead. My boy is dead. The son of peace died with cold steel in his guts.

Absalom, son of peace: I wish I had died instead of you. To this very day, I wish I had died.

L ATE AFTERNOON SUNLIGHT trickled into the hall where the king sat, his fingers pensively toying with a golden bowl of pearls. Out of habit, he took one of the pearls between his thumb and forefinger to rub the jewel against his teeth. He felt the gravelly rasp of authenticity, but it gave him no pleasure.

He was alone in the large chamber, his study and observatory. More and more in these days of his old age, he opted for solitude, though the time spent in his own company gave him no more comfort than that spent with his courtiers. He observed dust motes traced through the room by the slanting rays. Shuddering, he drew his cloak closer about his shoulders. Sunlight did little to drive the chill from his bones: The beams seemed only weary apparitions from ancient yesterdays. They offered neither warmth nor illumination.

The king stood to leave, sat again. To go, to stay; what difference would it make? The implacable tread of time ground everything under its feet; no choice abided. His hand strayed absently across the table by his chair, stumbling over the hilt of an old sword. His fingers tracing the familiar grip and jeweled haft, he remembered the first time he had ever held this sword in his hand...

The two women bowed before him. Behind him in the throne room gathered a crowd of petitioners, some from the hill country of Judah, some from as far north as Chinnereth. All of them were here because of him, because he was the king. He studied them, and knew he was not the only one who would pass judgment this day. They, too, were weighing evidence, choosing what to believe. Would he pass the test? Would the Lord, as He had promised, give him the wisdom to rule, to discern, to govern well?

To his right, slightly behind the women, a manservant held the disputed child in his arms. The baby began to cry. Looking sternly at the women, and praying silently for guidance, Solomon commanded that a sword be brought to him. A murmur rippled through the crowd, and the women both glanced up at him uncertainly, forgetting themselves momentarily in their surprise at his request. When he had the sword in hand, he said, "Bring the child to me." The manservant strode forward, the baby screaming in his grasp. Solomon stood, taking a firm grip on the gleaming weapon.

"I will cut this child in half," he pronounced in a ringing voice, above the frightened wails of the baby. "Then both of you may have half a child, and the dispute will be ended." Roughly he grasped the baby by one leg as if to yank him upward, but before he could do so, one of the women shrieked, "No! No, your majesty! Let her have the baby; only spare his life, I beg you!"

Slowly he lowered the sword and took the child from the manservant. He walked over to the woman who had cried out and was now sobbing on the floor as her adversary looked on uncomfortably. The king touched her shoulder, indicating that she should rise. Looking into this eyes, she wobbled to her feet.

Solomon placed the baby gently into her arms. "What true mother could sacrifice her own child's life, even if it meant not losing the baby to another? Your love for the child was stronger than your need to possess him; you have proved yourself his true mother."

A murmur from the crowd assured Solomon that he had passed the test. He was now their king and their judge.

The aging king smiled faintly in the shadow-filled study. Those had been heady days in Jerusalem, when he had con-solidated the laborious and bloody gains of his father's reign. He had taken up rule over all the territory from the Euphrates to Gaza, land which had cost David dearly — in the lives of soldiers, in horses, in mind-numbing marches. In innocence. In the blood of sons.

But the time of strife was past. God had blessed His people as never before, for the sake of His servant David's seed. The foundations of the temple were laid, the sweaty laborers having built in cedar and stone the dream his father had not lived to see.

Solomon rose and paced to a window affording a view of

the gardens and parks within the palace walls, and, in the middle distance, the temple, gilded and shadow-etched by the lingering light of day. The temple — the dwelling place of the Almighty. The palace — the dwelling place of the great king. *It was I who built them,* he reminded himself, *not my father David.*

The temple had required seven years to complete, the palace thirteen. It had been his calling to construct these monuments to the greatness of the God of his father. He had been raised for the job. Now, in retrospect, he found it odd — puzzling. All the expense and labor — for what end? No structure made by man's hands could withstand the unrelenting erosion of the years. *Surely one day,* he sighed hopelessly, *the temple, this house, these gardens, will be drifted over with the dust of neglect and disuse. The day will come when men will walk upon this place and not imagine that Solomon the King reigned here.*

Once foreign monarchs had fallen over themselves in haste to make alliance with the wise king. The fame of his splendid new palace, and the wealth and power it represented, had traveled far from Judah, and the entire world sent delegates to Israel, the crossroads of the world, to meet with Solomon and curry his good graces. With them came the richest offerings of their peoples — gold became nearly as common as dust in Jerusalem's streets, and even beggars prospered. Emissaries arrived from Phoenicia, from the islands of the Great Sea, from Egypt and the lands to the south, from Babylon and the lands between the rivers. And with them came the women.

He had his father's eye for women. He loved them all: the

dusky princesses of the south, the spirited chariot-maidens of the Hittites, the enigmatic, veiled daughters of Edom. But none was lovelier than the wife he first took, the daughter of the Pharaoh. Her skin was burnished to a luster in the golden hues of the Egyptian sun; her lips soft as the lotus petals floating in the pools of her father's courtyards; her dark, braided hair scented with delicate musk and jasmine. With her, and with the others, he sensed that the greatest miracle of God's creation found expression in the ecstasy between man and woman. It was a cup he joyfully drained again and again, an experience that moved him to poetic heights.

The scrolls — where are they? he wondered. He rose and crossed the carpeted floor to the far wall where large clay jars stood, illumined now by the sanguine glow of sunset shining through the hall's windows on the west. He paused, lifted the lid from one of them, and drew out a vellum scroll, yellowed with age and smelling of dust. As he carefully opened it, he began reading phrases from here and there:

I am the rose of Sharon, and the lily of the valleys...
I sat down under his shadow with great delight,
     and his fruit was sweet to my taste.
He brought me to the banqueting house,
     and his banner over me was love...
My beloved is mine, and I am his;
     he feedeth among the lilies.
Until the daybreak, and the shadows flee away,
     turn, my beloved...
Many waters cannot quench love,
     neither can the floods drown it...

Did I write these words? he murmured. *Why then am I not able to feel their tug within me? Why is the melody like the jangling doggerel of a drunken minstrel?*

Yet Solomon remembered when his songs were sung from Dan to Beersheba and beyond. The poetry of Zion's king had traveled to the east and west with the caravans, and by ship to lands and tongues far beyond the horizon. Likewise his words of wisdom were recorded and circulated, prized for their erudition and cogency. It pleasured him deeply in those days to drink at wisdom's fountain, to trace onto papyrus the bright filigrees of his insights.

Was it possible, still, to summon to his command this gift? Perhaps even now he could find solace in his pen. By articulating his despair, might he not weaken its potency? Going to his writing table, he scrabbled through the debris littering its surface to find a scrap of clean papyrus. He took a stylus, first dipping it in the water bowl, then stroking it on the dried ink-cake. Then he held it, poised, above the papyrus.

Nothing came. Silence mocked him scornfully from the void in his soul. The stylus dropped from his fingers, leaving ink splatters on the papyrus. His face fell into his hands.

What has robbed me of vision? he wondered. *My father — that old man with blood up to his elbows — he died with peace in his heart and a song on his lips. Despite the death of sons, he found words to mitigate the pain of his waning days. Something made his music dance on the page. Why does it elude me? To the end his songs were vivid with emotion, while mine were merely clever. He, raised as a shepherd, had the singing spirit of a poet; while I, raised as a*

♦

prince, have only a philosopher's soul. Music is the ointment I crave — but it lies beyond my grasp, and knowledge offers no comfort.

Unbidden, a line from one of his father's songs floated into his mind. But it was a dirge of grief and longing: *My God, my God, why hast thou forsaken me?* Leaning back and closing his eyes, he softly quoted to himself the passage:

Why art thou so far from helping me, and from the words of my groaning? O my God, I cry in the daytime, but thou hearest not, and in the night season, and am not silent. But thou art holy, O thou that inhabitest the praises of Israel. Our fathers trusted in thee; they trusted in thee, and were not confounded.

He opened his eyes, looking into one of the graying corners of the hall. There, squatting in the deepening shadows, sat the likeness of a many-breasted fertility goddess. Which one of his wives had placed the ugly totem there? Impossible to say — for so many gods had found their way to his palace...

Solomon was reclining on a spice-filled cushion beside a quiet pool strewn with lotuses. A concubine sat nearby, playing softly on her harp and singing one of his own newly composed love songs. Into the garden wandered his youngest wife, a charming princess from Sidon, a pout dimpling the corners of her pretty mouth.

"What's the matter, my pet?" he inquired solicitously, for he was in an expansive mood.

"My lord king, have I not been a faithful and devoted wife to you?"

"Why — yes, yes. Who claims otherwise?"

"No one, lord, only — only, I would ask a favor."

He smiled. "Ask it at once. I can bear no more of this frowning from such a lovely face."

"My lord king: I've been away from my homeland three years. I'm happy at your palace, but it would make my life in Jerusalem more pleasant if I had some of my own people to converse with — so I could hear my native tongue once again."

"My sweet, this isn't such a great thing to ask. Of course you may bring friends here. I will send an envoy to fetch them, if you like."

"Thank you, lord. And...and also..." She looked wistfully over her shoulder, biting her lip as though afraid to say more.

"Out with it, my dear."

She laughed — a light, twinkling, quick laugh, calculated to gratify her audience. "I hesitate to ask, but — you see, while my friends are here, they will surely be required to pray to idols of Ashteroth, the goddess of our people."

Solomon looked carefully at her. The wide, imploring set of her eyes was unmistakable. "Ah...I see..." He felt a twinge somewhere within.

He could, if he chose, deny her request. It would be rash to openly invite idols into Jerusalem, into the palace. It would arouse the anger of the priests, and their anger could be troublesome.

But to deny her — that, too, would bring discomfort. She would certainly not do or say anything openly; such things were simply not done. But there were other ways: a certain coldness, a certain reserve, feigned sickness at certain times.

No, he could never live with that. At least the priests did not have to be faced daily.

"My dear, as long as the graven images are not displayed prominently in my house — you may do as you wish. Do you understand?"

She frowned, then suddenly brightened, and rained such a flurry of hugs and kisses on him that he laughingly remonstrated in mock protest, before dismissing her to carry out her plans.

Around a harem, nothing spreads so rapidly as the hint of favoritism. Before long Solomon was besieged daily by supplicating women, wheedling from him permission to do as the others did. He began to regret his first leniency, so vexing their constant nagging. Still, acceding to their pleas seemed easiest and harmless. Eventually, incense from a hundred altars wafted cloyingly through his house. Scarcely could he walk ten paces without encountering some totem or shrine to one or another of the women's fancied deities. He had either to wink at them all, or disappoint and anger his many wives.

The altars did not content them, however. They soon began requesting his attendance at their ceremonies. Not for a moment did he believe in the efficacy of such idol worship, but thinking himself gracious, he humored their benighted mysticism.

The old king wondered: *Was it during those days I first began to feel empty? Did the vanity of my life grow from the seed of that first concession to a pretty pout?*

Solomon had attempted to quiet the disturbing vacuum in his soul with activity and achievement. He continually inspected and improved his armories, his barracks, his stables; he built new gardens, walls, and vineyards. He reassured himself of the self-sufficiency of his domain. He delved again into study of philosophies and human nature. With the ablest sages he could gather he argued metaphysical propositions for hours and wrote reams of observations on the human condition. With one voice the world lauded the greatness of his mind, the magnificence of his kingdom, the justness of his rule.

Yet the cavity in his heart ached the worse. His doubts and misgivings mocked his best efforts. The single lack in his life spoke with a voice louder than the thousand-throated praises of his subjects. It beggared the splendor of his treasury.

I must turn again to David's God, he thought, struggling to shake off the feelings of foolishness and failure that had haunted all his most recent stumbling attempts to invoke Yahweh's blessing. In his mind he strained to push further back, to a time long ago, to the days of his youth when he had worshiped the Creator. He had sought His wisdom and been blessed abundantly. Would the Lord now grant him a heart of peace? Or had too much time passed? In his search for pleasure and wisdom he had lost the habit of piety. Could it be regained?

Darkness reigned in the hall, the twilight having subsided into inevitable night. Still the king sat, consumed with his pondering. He was surrounded in the room by the spoils of success. But now, in the blackness, they were lost from sight — empty, meaningless...gone.

And We Beheld His Glory

 OW, WHERE'S that oak planking? I had it here just the other — there! "Son, come here. Help me carry this planking to my workbench."

"Yes, Father."

"That's fine. Just put it down there beside the table. Good. Thank you, Son — that was a help."

"Yes, Sir."

Rabbi wants a doorway. It should be oak. These planks look true. Big knot there, but it's tight. Have to make sure the dowels are on the sides of it. Never drill into an oak knot; good way to break a drill. Yes, these should smooth out nicely. I'll make Aaron an entrance that will be the pride of his house.

"What are you doing there, Joshua?"

"I'm making something, Father. Just like you do."

"Fine, then." First thing is to plane these edges...

He looks so intent, squatting there in the sawdust, playing

◆

with the wood chips and shavings, placing them just so. Frowning as he concentrates, like a master carver. Different from other children, even in his play I think, somehow entering into it more deeply than any child I've ever seen. He becomes what he's doing...

Better watch what I'm doing. Nearly planed my thumb. "Joshua, I need your help. Stand this plank lengthwise against the other side of the table, would you? As I plane them, you could stand each one up, couldn't you?"

"Yes, Father."

"What's that you put together over there?"

"Oh, it's...it's supposed to be a little wooden man."

"Why the frown, son?"

"Well, I...I think I could have done it better. It doesn't seem right yet."

Now to drill the holes for the dowel pins. I like oak, though it's hard to work sometimes. A stubborn wood, but when something's done right in oak, there's nothing better, to my mind.

What goes on in that head of his, I wonder — when he gets that thoughtful, distant look on his face? Maybe listening for something only he can hear. Like a call, or an echo from far away. Other voices. Sometimes when I ask him to help me, or his mother calls him to the table, it's as if he's been interrupted — as if we're intruders. I wonder if he hears things from the past. Faint reverberations of an angel's song, or the distant screams of toddling boys ripped from their mothers' arms in Bethlehem.

Now look what I've done — gone and split this pin! Have to make another now. That's what I get for woolgather-

ing. A gentler touch, that's what's needed here. You can't force oak.

"Joshua, I hear your friends calling you. I think you ought to go and play with them."

"Reuben! Simon! I'm here, in the shop! Wait, I'm coming!"

How long, I wonder, before he hears the first sneers about his parentage? How long before the children he runs and laughs with today begin to repeat the things their parents have whispered when Mary and I pass them in the streets? And who would believe me if I tried to explain? Carpenters aren't supposed to have visions. No, people see only that quiet wood carver Joseph, unwilling as usual to make a fuss. Sometimes I think marrying her was the first brave thing I've ever done — maybe the only brave thing I'll ever do. But would anyone believe me if I told them?

There. That should be wide enough. Let's see...yes. Now to find a piece for making a couple of cross-braces.

Look there. The children gathered round him as if around a crackling fire on a cold night. Warming to the light within him, laughing with him at an animated jest. He gives himself to them, spends himself recklessly upon them. Why? And why do I feel as if I ought to be learning from him, as if I ought to peer deeply into his eyes until I understand the secrets and promises hidden there? And why do I also fear doing so?

I'll take this over to Aaron's house to trim. Want to be sure to match the curve of the planks to the curve of his archway. Say...where's my small chisel? I could do some scrollwork or some decorative carving around the door

frame. *Wonder if he'd like that? But first, let's get the bottom
evened up. Then I'll need to smooth it all down...*

*I wonder about him. His rabbi says he asks amazing
questions, and then, when the answer comes, looks quizzical
as if expecting something more. A boy of five, confounding
the rabbis?*

*And how can I help him? I am no scholar. I am merely
his guardian, and as disquieted by his enigmatic wisdom, his
innocent complexity, as anyone else. Someday he will ask
the right questions of the wrong people, and their response
will be untempered by the love I carry in my breast for him.
Even now, I sometimes think he is treading a path that carries
him toward some dire conflict. But how to voice such things
to a boy of five? How to explain what I can scarcely put into
thought?*

*Mary knows, I think. She carries a burden in her heart far
heavier than what she carried in her womb. When she
watches over his bed at night, the battle between joy and
sadness is played out upon her face. She looks at him with a
gaze different than that spent upon James or the other
children. In some unseen way she shares his anointing, as he
shared her life-giving blood.*

*Ah...done. Smooth as the cheek of a child. And that knot
adds character, I fancy, rather than detracts. Aaron will like
this door, I warrant.*

*Wipe off the dust. Yes, if you want a thing to last, you've
got to start with good stock. For a job like this, give me oak
every time.*

YOU CAN LEARN a lot about people by watching them eat and drink. Since I am, by trade, a purveyor of food-stuffs, I have had ample opportunities for examination. I have seen religious men — men who scrupulously keep the Law — betray the greed in their souls by their petulance when a favored delicacy runs short. I have seen men who were purported to be wise made fools by too much wine. And I have seen poor farmers — tilling rocky land that barely supports their families — who regularly invite widows to their tables on a day of celebration. Such charity comes dear.

Wedding feasts are my favorite occasions. The complex blend of happiness, anxiety, relief (of the bride's father, if she is well-married), and anticipation tell much about a family and a community.

When Reuben bar-Simeon asked me to preside over the wedding feast of his eldest son, I was unsure how to respond.

Reuben and I had been friends since boyhood, and at one time I felt almost as if his son were one of my own. Indeed, for some time it seemed inevitable that he should become my son. You see, my daughter Anna doted on Asher. Countless the times I saw them making eyes at each other, playing at love, grinning together when they thought no one saw. But then when Asher became betrothed to Lydia instead... A child's pain is multiplied a hundred times over in the breast of her father. So I hesitated long before I agreed to preside at the feast.

I thought I had made all the necessary preparations. I had selected the cheeses with my usual care, secured olives at the peak of succulence, baked the bread in my own ovens. Everything seemed adequate to me, though I confess I did not relish the prospect of sharing my prized wines with those who caused my Anna such hurt. But friendship dies hard, and I had agreed, after all.

On the morning of the celebration day, I began growing apprehensive about the sufficiency of our provisions. I was aware that Reuben was well-known in Galilee, but it seemed that everyone who had ever met him had come today to Cana. If Reuben were unable to adequately serve his guests and was so dishonored, nothing in heaven or earth would ever convince him I had not embarrassed him intentionally. I swear to you, such was not my wish. But the wedge driven between us would be final — immovable.

Hurriedly I sent Lucius, my chief servant, to the market to secure such additional supplies as might be available, while I hurried back to my storehouse to bring more wine. To my chagrin, I had only two more jars, and these hardly fit to be served at a wedding feast. Still, I did not know what else to do, since the feast was already beginning, and there was no other large store of wine in the village. Cursing my lack of foresight, I had the jars loaded and carted back to Reuben's house.

Just as I feared, all Galilee seemed to be gathered around Reuben's table. I was an island of gloom amid the sea of hilarity. Each time one of my servants brought out another tray of food or another pitcher of wine, I winced inwardly.

Late in the afternoon I saw one of the serving girls pluck at Lucius' sleeve and whisper urgently in his ear. Feeling the blood drain into my stomach, I arose and went to them. "Master!" hissed Lucius. "We are out of wine! Still people linger, and we have nothing else to serve them!"

I was numb with the shame of my mismanagement. What could I do? As I stood paralyzed by embarrassment, a woman approached. "Good sirs," she said softly, "my son is able to help." I looked at her in puzzlement, then over to her son, a youngish man of nondescript appearance. My first impression was that he seemed discomfited, like a child called upon by his father to recite for guests.

Then everything changed. He looked closely at me, and I swear to you he immediately knew my perplexity. And he knew deeper — knew the love that lived yet in my heart for Reuben, despite the wound dealt my daughter; knew the dilemma spinning inside me; knew the fear I felt, the fear of losing a friend forever.

He motioned for Lucius to follow him, and went off toward the storeroom. His mother called after them needlessly: "Do whatever my son tells you!"

I returned to the head table, feeling as a child feels lying in his mother's lap. All would be well. Just as the first empty cup clumped down upon the board, Lucius arrived, his eyes wide as a startled cat's, holding a bowl out to me. I took it and sipped its contents. Wine glided over my tongue like honey, curling satisfyingly about my palate. I have heard the Greeks speak of Bacchus, their god of wine. If a god made wine, it would taste like what I now sipped.

I handed the bowl back to Lucius, indicating he should serve the guests.

Then I sought out Reuben and his son. "It is customary," I reminded them, "to serve the better wine first. Later, when tastes are less acute, one brings out the lesser wine. But now your guests shall taste the best wine of all. Your feast will be the talk of Galilee."

The woman's son came out of the storeroom, paused, and winked at me. Then he turned and left, mingling with the crowd. I arose to go to him, but various guests kept detaining me and I did not see him again.

I hear he travels around the countryside teaching. Some say he performs miracles, as in the days of the prophets. I never was one to believe in miracles overmuch, until that day in Cana. For Lucius told me they had filled the stone jars with water, and dipped out the rich red wine in its place. How else could such things be?

Some who've heard him say that he has spoken about new wine and old wineskins. Others say the Pharisees accuse him of being a drunkard. I do not think so. I think he is a master vintner, sent to choose the choicest grapes from the vineyard.

Sent from where, you ask? I am afraid to answer. But I have never forgotten the taste of his wine. I remember with my tongue...and with my soul.

WE HAD JUST LEFT Jerusalem on the run. The Sanhedrin had come harrowingly near to stoning him, and us with him, because he wouldn't answer them.

Oh, he gave them answers, all right — just not the answers they wanted. And for his trouble they were ready to kill him. We got out of there, but I wasn't sure how, and a boulder of fear weighted my belly.

We were with him out in the desert country between Beth-nimrah and Beth-haram when messengers from Mary and Martha found us and said Lazarus was on his death bed. When the messengers left, however, he seemed to indicate the sickness wasn't serious. I was relieved, not because of concern for Lazarus, but because I trembled at the thought of going back to Bethany, so close to Jerusalem, after our narrow escape.

Two days later he said to us, "We're going back to Judea."

"Going back?" we protested. "After what just happened at

the temple?" Even Peter blanched at the prospect of returning into the clutches of the Sanhedrin.

It was no use, of course. Looking back, it seems laughable that we would even try to dissuade him from a path he had chosen. As well might sheep lead the shepherd.

"Lazarus is dead," he told us. "Let us go to him."

The words sank in slowly. No one spoke. It was clear he was determined to go back. I cast my lot, however desperate: "Let us go and die with him," I told the others.

When we got close to Bethany, it looked as though all Jerusalem had come out to console Mary and Martha. I became even more nervous, and had recurring visions of being snatched by the temple guards and marched to the nearest stone pit.

Surrounded by wailing mourners, Mary fell at his feet sobbing. "If you had been here, my brother would not have died," she complained. I wondered about this myself. Lazarus was a special friend who had often comforted us on our travels. It seemed callous to allow this thing to happen if he were capable of preventing it, as I felt him to be.

But Lazarus had now been in the tomb four days. Had we run this ridiculous gauntlet for no purpose whatever?

He looked around the throng for a moment, saw the pain of Mary and Martha, saw our discomfort and befuddlement. He raised his face toward heaven...and wept.

He wept. To this day I have remembered the look in his eyes. Perhaps he grieved not so much for the death of Lazarus, nor for the bereavement of Mary and Martha — though I know in my heart that these things caused him sadness. No, it seemed to me that day (and the certainty has grown stronger since) that those eyes of his, which had seen the births of suns and moons and found these good, now gazed on the very essence of all that was wrong and ill and painful, and knew death for the hideous perversion it was. He saw our pathetic confusion, and he wept. Perhaps he even saw the unborn millions who would come into this world and know its hurt, come face to face with its disappointments, impale themselves upon its broken promises. He wept, and each tear was a drop of absolution for those stumbling mortals who would follow him to his ultimate destination.

I saw his tears chase one another down the temples of his upturned face. I suppose that is why I followed him. His tears were a fountain in my desert, a confirmation of my choice… an anointing.

You have heard, of course, what happened next, after he approached the tomb where Lazarus lay — how he stood in the stench of four days' death-rot, and brought back life into decaying flesh. It raised the hackles on the back of my neck to hear his clear voice that could reach Lazarus's dead ears…to feel the irresistible power in his words, and to know I was seeing the impossible occur. And you have heard how so many witnessed this, and believed in him.

But that scene has never replaced, in my mind's eye, the powerful sight of his tears welling up from the springs of living water within him, spilling onto the dust — drops of clemency and grace, more cleansing than the blood sprinkled with hyssop on the Mercy Seat. He saw us in all our squalor and misery and fear, and loved us. So he wept.

He wept.

T HE PHYSICIANS SAY I haven't long to live. What matter is that to me? I, of all men, should not fear death, for I have met its Master.

The first time I saw him, Mary came dragging him in by the hand, demanding that Martha get him something to eat. I assumed he was the latest of her infatuations; she was forever falling in love with men who had the smell of exotic places in their clothing. It soon became apparent he did not fit that mold — his speech betrayed his Galilean upbringing, his hands bore the hard calluses of a tradesman.

I was drawn to him as a calf is drawn to its mother's side by her lowing. I asked him where his home was, and he smiled wistfully — or was it painfully? — and said he had none to speak of. Despite his apparent poverty, I had an obscure sense I was in the presence of a great teacher, perhaps even a prophet.

He seemed to enjoy that visit with us, so I invited him to

come again to Bethany. He came often, the next year or two. We all were eager for his return visits, but I think Mary was most so. She seemed to *need* his words, to long for conversation with him and his blessing. Indeed, I saw my wayward sister transformed by him. I had despaired of ever curing her of her profligate ways, and nearly resigned myself to seeing her die one day in the stone pit.

When she came to know Jesus of Nazareth, she became reflective. She learned to seek more than gratification of the flesh, to thirst for a higher good than earthly happiness. She loved much because she had been forgiven much. For this, if for no other reason, he won my appreciation.

But there was more. He was a man of wholeness, within and without. He is the only man I ever knew whose words and actions were the same. Indeed, the one gave strength and meaning to the other. Being a merchant, I study people, for they are my stock and trade. All men, if observed long enough and in enough different circumstances, will betray the dross hiding beneath the golden exteriors they present to the world. Take, for example, the rabbi Joseph bar-Levi. He extols the holiness of God loud and long in the synagogue on the Sabbath. His words are impressive and eloquent. But next day in my shop, he curses under his breath because I won't sell him my goods for less than cost.

And, I must confess, after I met the Nazarene I began to notice things about myself — a peevishness when my generosity went unnoticed; a resentment for the lack of appreciation I felt was due from my sisters — little things no one but I could know. When he would come into the house, hot and dusty and blinking from the sunlight, I might offer him a cool

drink of a special wine I had saved for the occasion. His smile
would be quick and honest, his face grateful as he quenched
his road-thirst. I would wait, hoping to receive a compliment
on the wine, an inquiry on its origin, some praise for my
thoughtfulness. But no — just a smile of thanks, and the
uncomplicated enjoyment of slaking his thirst. And sometimes
a tiny flicker of a smile from the corner of his eye — as though
he knew, understood, forgave and dismissed my petulance —
while never diminishing his enjoyment of the cup.

He made me a friend. And I loved him.

Once, when I became seriously ill, my sisters wanted to
send for him immediately. I told them not to worry — it was
not the first time I had been sick and recovered. Perhaps they
sensed what I did not. Later they told me I languished in a
delirium for three days, and each day one of them waited by
the road, anxiously hoping to see him approach in the
distance. But he did not come.

All I can tell of the time between time is that I slept. A
darkness beyond darkness enfolded me, and I slept. And then
a voice was calling to me, a call I could not refuse. A fire
kindled in my chest, slowly grew in intensity, spread to my
fingers and toes, quickening my limbs, banishing the tentacles
of cold that bound me. I saw a bright light, and a familiar form
silhouetted in its glow. The voice pierced the clinging mist
about my head, penetrated my brain, infused my body with
imperative strength. I awoke in a hole in the side of a hill. A
foul stench besmirched the air. I realized later that it must
have been the odor of my own death.

I tottered out of the tomb, staggering under the weight of
the bandages and spices. As I limped blinking into the

sunlight, a great shout went up. It seemed a thousand people stood on the hillside. But I heard only one voice — his voice, the voice that awakened me from the cold sleep. With tears still wet on his cheeks, he smiled, held out his hands to me, and began to unwrap the grave clothes.

He fell out of favor with the priests in Jerusalem. Perhaps he never was in favor with them, I do not know. Later, I heard they were seeking my life, along with his. After all, I was a walking endorsement of his power! I wonder if they intended to slay everyone who had been in Bethany that day, and had seen what happened. Perhaps so.

When they crucified him, my sisters wept bitterly, but I heard the echo of his call in my entombed soul, and I kept my own counsel. How could they think death would contain him? Yet, I had no power to lift aside the heavy sorrow that draped them like a shroud of lead. I suppose I was afraid of their grief — they seemed so certain. But on the third day, when Mary rushed in with her news, I was the only one in the room who did not doubt her sanity.

I have followed the Way all these years since. How could I do anything else? How could I, to whom He had once given life, refuse Him? I am His, despite anything Caiaphas, Pilate, Caesar, or Satan himself might do. Soon I shall be reunited with Him. Again I'll hear the call that awakened me and shall awaken all mankind.

Let death come. I do not fear it. I've known death before — and I have met its Master.

L EMUEL THE MILLER approached and stood before me, unwilling now to look up, to let me see the hatred in his eyes. He knew that, if I chose, I could tax the very wheels on his cart and the hooves of the beast drawing it.

I sat on the dais, behind my table, armed bailiffs flanking me. How I gloated at the impotent stance of this miserable, dusty wretch! Perhaps now Lemuel would regret the taunts with which he had tortured me during my childhood. Oh yes, I remembered — how well I remembered!

"Come along, little Zaccheus," they would say. "What's the matter, tiny one? Can't you keep up?" Their laughter slapped at me, stinging like a lash, bringing acid tears of anger to my eyes. How I hated them then — and hated myself for my own helplessness! More than anything I longed to be not just as big as they, but bigger — to be able to gaze down and laugh at *their* frailty...to taunt and humiliate *them.*

Time had passed — and I found a way to do it.

I always had a quick head for business, and sums were second nature to me. My father had a profitable trade in Jericho, and through the years I found that I was able to take small amounts of money and judiciously invest them to return larger amounts. By the time I reached full manhood, I had been managing all my father's accounts for years. When he died, I was more than able to turn a handsome profit on the sale of the family business. With the proceeds, I obtained through various means the appointment as tax collector for the Jericho district. Certainly there was money to be made for me in securing funds for the Emperor, but the monetary rewards were secondary to the emotional gratification.

For now I had power. I had my hand on the purse-strings of those very men who had so tormented me as a boy. Did they cause me misery by calling me names? I dealt them far worse at the toll-booth. Did their ceaseless cruel jibes drain the joy out of my childhood? I slowly siphoned their life-blood into my counting-bins. And all with Caesar's blessing and protection. Oh, I exulted in watching them come and cower before me!

"Well now, Lemuel! It has been a good year, has it not? No doubt you prosper, grinding grain for the farmers. Surely you cannot begrudge Caesar his small due. What? No answer? Well then, let's see...shall we say — ten drachmae?"

Now he looked up and spoke, his eyes bulging from

his head. "Ten drachmae! You filthy…"

"You were saying, miller?" I snarled, daring him to continue.

I was a small child who had grown up to become an even smaller man. So small, in fact, that I had begun to collapse inwardly upon myself, like a pomegranate rotting from within. I had grown vicious and vindictive, deriving less and less satisfaction from my revenge. Thus it is with those whose preoccupation is themselves.

I had heard stories about the rabbi who was gathering a following in the north country. I'd heard rumors of amazing feats — demons cast out, sickness healed. Some of the ruffians in the district of Galilee were even making noises about this one being the Messiah who would re-establish Israel and purge the land of the Roman infidels and their lackeys. Of course, I wasn't eager for that to happen. Every few years or so some rabble-rouser would gather a band of renegades and run off into the desert to organize a militia. These pitiful characters always wound up nailed to a cross.

But this fellow had in his entourage a certain Matthew Levi, a tax collector from somewhere around Capernaum. The typical Roman-hating rebels would as soon slit a publican from chin to navel as look at him. To them, we tax collectors were traitors to the Jewish Cause, whatever that was. So why should a publican follow a zealot?

One day a crowd gathered outside my counting house. In curiosity I went outside — cautiously, for a publican can never be too careful. From the scene that greeted me, one

would have thought the Syrian Legion was marching
through town in full-dress regalia. People were lining up
along the main road, elbowing each other for space. I
heard snatches of conversation as they hurried past, and
picked up that this rabbi from Galilee was on his way to
town — and that he had healed old Timeus's blind son,
who used to sit and beg just outside the city gate.

But because of my stature I could see nothing. I
wanted to get closer to the roadside, but thought better of
forcing my way through the jostling crowd. Surely some
dagger in the roiling mob would like nothing better than to
drink my blood, and my bodyguards were elsewhere.

A large sycamore overhung the road nearby. The
lowest branch was higher than I could have reached while
standing on another's shoulders. Nevertheless it was my
only chance. I glanced quickly around — all eyes were on
the road — then wrapped my arms and legs around its
smooth, piebald circumference and began climbing like a
schoolboy.

When I finally reached the first branch, he was just
coming abreast of the counting house. Wading through the
shouting crowd, he happened to glance up. Our eyes met,
and he stopped. I stared back at him, feeling somehow
that I recognized his face. Someone who had looked up at
me from my collecting table? A dimly remembered friend?
A boyhood enemy?

The attention of the crowd was shifting toward me. I
must have cut a rather amusing figure — a grown man in a
brocade robe, turban askew, sweating on a sycamore limb.
I heard smirks and sneers at the sight of the Emperor's

chief publican roosting like a treed cat. The blood burned in my cheeks.

He, too, smiled, but not in derision. He seemed to be honestly amused, as one might be at a harmless prank. He turned to the crowd and asked my name. "Rabbi," some wag called out, "that is Zaccheus, our chief tax collector, and *a very big man* in Jericho!" The mob roared with mirth.

But I scarcely heard them, for he continued smiling at me acceptingly. "Zaccheus," he said, "please come down. I am hungry. I should like to dine at your house today."

The silence was utter. This one whom some believed to be Daniel's apocalyptic "Son of Man" was not only speaking to a traitor, but actually wishing to break bread with him. It was all too big a bite for this crowd to swallow.

A big, rough-looking man was with the rabbi, and I saw him staring white-eyed first at the rabbi, then at me, then back again to the rabbi, as if he could not believe his ears. Nor did I know what to say.

The silence continued as I slid awkwardly down the trunk to the ground, then walked toward him. He hadn't taken his eyes off me, nor did the amused smile leave his face.

As he and his band of followers — a ragtag lot they were — entered my house, I scanned them carefully, trying to see which one might be the publican. Each face regarded me warily for a moment, then turned away. Only two returned my attentions — the rabbi, of course, and another whose look seemed to promise things I could not imagine. His eyes twinkled as I stared at the dusty, weathered robe he wore — brocaded silk. I must have had a question on my face, for he gripped me lightly on the shoulder and said simply, "You will see." This, I soon learned, was Matthew.

As we reclined at table, the rabbi's speech fell upon my ears like rain on drought-parched soil. I did not understand all of what I heard, but his words sounded gently inevitable, like the rising tide which slowly lifts even the heaviest-laden vessel from the sand. Perhaps he thought he addressed only his twelve companions, but his words struck my heart like diamond-tipped darts. My table had become his lectern, and my life his text.

He spoke of God's kingdom which was soon to come, but his was no saber-rattling war council. He spoke of giving wealth to the poor, but I heard no castigation of the rich. And he spoke of love — love for one's enemies. I suppose if I had watched his disciples' faces I would have seen them glance my way at the mention of the enemy. But I looked at his face, and saw in it — through a coruscation of tears — the faces of all those I had wronged in my pathetic malevolence.

My soul, which I thought impervious to tenderness, was disarmed.. Here was balm to salve the wounds I had vainly tried to stanch with spite.

Finally he spoke of death. He spoke of falling to the ground as does a seed, and of new life rising from the husk. He spoke of laying aside cherished possessions, and of the freedom that results in such abdication of oneself.

This seemed to make the twelve uneasy, but as he spoke, I knew what I must do.

I stood, and heard my voice spill out into the house, seeming very loud, juxtaposed as it was with his quiet, confident tone. Everyone, myself included, was startled, for he had spoken, as I have said, not to me, but to his followers.

"Rabbi," I said, "I am a greedy man, and a hateful one. I have done wrong to many, and hurt them, and I cannot undo that. But I will do what I can. This day I will liquidate my possessions and distribute half to the poor. With the other half I will repay fourfold any man whose goods I have extorted."

I wanted to say more, but the words hung in my throat. I was rendered mute by the approval in his eyes. I sat down.

There was a long silence. I noticed Matthew smiling at the floor, nodding slightly.

"Today," said the rabbi, "salvation has come to this house. Zaccheus, your faith proves that you are, after all, a true son of Abraham."

I felt overwhelmed with relief, as if an iron chain I had been dragging had suddenly changed to straw.

I followed them that evening to the edge of town and watched until the tiny procession wound around a bend in the road leading up into the hills. Turning to go back, I saw Lemuel approaching, wearily driving his cart before him.

"Lemuel," I said. He drew up short, and looked away from the gaunt flanks of his donkey. When he saw me, resentment froze his face into a sullen mask. His eyes darted right and left, looking for my henchmen.

"Lemuel, I have something that belongs to you." I handed him a pouch. He took it warily, hefting it enough to hear the coins jingling inside.

"What sort of publican trick is this?" he growled.

I made no answer, standing very still in the road, not taking my eyes from his. After a moment he could resist no longer; he gingerly opened the pouch and gasped, uncomprehending. Then he poured the contents into his palm. I saw his lips move silently as he counted the silver. In a moment he stared at me, incredulous. "Thirty-nine drachmae!" he breathed.

"Well, Caesar must have his one-drachma tax; I cannot do anything about that. But I wanted to return to you with interest what I stole this morning. And here—" I removed a gold ring from my finger, holding it out to him. "Perhaps this will make the tax less odious."

He made no move, continuing to stare at me as at a lunatic. Finally I dropped the ring into his cart, chuckling.

"Take the ring, miller, as well as the money," I said.

"What— what has come over you, Zaccheus? A tax collector...returning tax with interest? Such could never happen!"

"Actually, friend Lemuel," I said, leaving him to puzzle, "it has."

I WAS EXPECTING a good week — festival weeks always were. The usual crowds of pilgrims would eagerly throng into Jerusalem from their faraway little villages. They would be the main source of my trade, for there is something about the anonymity granted by distance from home that causes men to seek out my kind. They would do things this week that they would not dream of doing within a day's journey of their homes. It is ironic, I suppose, that they come to the holy city, perhaps hoping to contract holiness from exposure to the temple, and at the same time find themselves still driven by less noble urges. Still, it was my opportunity to earn good money, and I was prepared to take advantage.

I was not particularly surprised when a Pharisee approached me — several Pharisees were regular customers of mine. Apparently, the weight of righteousness became at times too heavy to bear, and they required my ministrations to maintain their stamina. These amused me most. When they came in, they averted their eyes from mine. I could tell they felt shame for themselves — and loathing for me, but I had long ago lost any concern for such niceties as self-respect.

Since that day, eternities ago, when I was abandoned to the random cruelties of the world by those who should have cared for me, I had learned that survival was the only law, and survival took no notice of sentiment. I had hated myself far too long to waste time on concern for others. As long as their coin was good, their motives were of no consequence.

This fellow came in and tossed the usual amount of currency on the table. He had been to me before, but as I looked up at him through the heavy, musk-laden air of my room, his face seemed different. Instead of stealing furtive glances at my ankles, then blushing and looking away, he regarded me almost boldly, with a sardonic smile playing at the corners of his lips. I had observed too many men of his type not to be puzzled; but, as I have said, his money was in order, and that was my main concern.

A few moments later a troop of temple guards burst through my door. I screamed and rolled off my couch, cowering and covering myself with bedclothes. Far from being frightened, the Pharisee, apparently expecting this interruption, laughed and nonchalantly rearranged his clothing. "Take her away," he snapped, and as the guards dragged me, kicking and screaming, out the door, I saw him gather his coins from the table and put them back in his purse.

They hauled me down to the temple, through the crowds of festival-goers and curious bystanders. All turned to see this strange sight: a woman, barely clad, dragged through the streets by keepers of the law and of worship.

"Why?" I screamed, "Why do you do this? Has my presence been a secret to you until now, that you suddenly descend upon me? Have your masters found fault with my services, that today they pronounce sentence upon me?"

One of the guards turned and struck me on the mouth, commanding me to be quiet. I went the rest of the way in terrified silence.

There was a group of people in the outer court of the temple, gathered around a rabbi who was seated on a low wall. The guards pushed me through these strangers and tossed me in a heap at the feet of this man. Sobbing, I crouched down, covering myself as best I could.

There was a long hush. A number of Pharisees and scribes had quietly materialized and encircled the rabbi, as though in response to a prearranged signal. Now one of them nervously cleared his throat, glanced toward the others as if to find his cue, and said to the rabbi, "We caught this woman in the very act of committing adultery. The Law says she should die. What do you say?"

Someone in the crowd muttered, "Where is he with whom she did this thing? Surely she did not commit adultery alone, and the Law says they must both die." Several Pharisees looked sharply in the direction of the voice, and I did not hear it again.

There was silence once more. After a moment, I looked up at the rabbi — and felt myself to be falling into an unimaginably deep well, so profound was his gaze. I tried vainly to better cover myself, tugging at the few scant shreds of clothing I clutched. But I think if I had been robed from head to foot, and veiled besides, I would still have felt naked under his eyes, exposed to his view in a way that made attempts at concealment irrelevant. I knew my sin, knew the entire weight of its filth — and knew he knew it too. Yet, unbelievably, he did not turn from me in disgust. He did not spit on me and consign me to the stone pit, which, at this moment, even I knew I deserved. Instead he looked away briefly, seemed to blink back tears, and quietly began to write in the dusty earth with his finger.

At length, someone spoke into the silence. "Well? What do you say? Does she deserve death, or not?"

I glanced up at the one who spoke. He was staring at the rabbi as a wolf might stare at a lamb, or like a jackal eyeing the lion on the kill. It came to me in a flash that this entire spectacle was aimed not at me, but at this humble itinerant who still sat as he had been, quietly moving his finger in the dirt. They were after *him*, and I was merely an instrument, a lure to be used to bait a trap, then discarded when its usefulness was gone.

For a long moment I didn't breathe. I could smell the sweat of the crowd as it mingled with the stench of my own fear. There was no movement but the soft tracing of the rabbi's finger in the dust. I sensed that the entire universe was paused, waiting to hear what he would say.

Finally he raised his eyes resolutely to the Pharisees and scribes, swallowed, and said very quietly, "Whoever of you has never sinned — Let him cast the first stone." His eyes held theirs for a long time, until, one by one, they each looked away. The rabbi then turned his face downward and again stretched his finger to make patterns in the dirt.

I was afraid to move or speak. I felt that doom hovered over us all like a bird of prey. Then I heard the shuffling of feet. The crowd was drifting away in ones and twos. The older ones seemed to be the first to grasp his meaning and take their leave, but presently everyone left except the rabbi, still drawing in the dust, and myself. He looked at me, glanced quickly around the court, then back at me.

"Where are your accusers?" he asked. I thought I saw the trace of a smile in his eyes.

"There is no one...no one here but you, sir," I stammered.

"Neither do I condemn you. Go..." he said. I rose to leave.

"...and leave your life of sin."

I stood pinioned to the ground. His last phrase burned in me like an ice-cold blade. I felt myself alternately blanching and blushing. He knew who I really was, and yet he asked me to become clean, as though that were a possibility for me. Indeed, he expected it of me! But what fountain could cleanse such a one as I, who had sold my own integrity to the highest bidder, and then sold and resold it again and again? Did he not know that I was not my own, that I was no longer in control of my destiny, that my dignity did not matter anymore? That my soul had been slain on the altar of human necessity, sacrificed to the demons of lust as barter for continued existence? Surely with those eyes, deep as the seas, he would see that I could never be free from my guilt. And still he stood, staring at me, his command etched as clearly in his look as if chiseled in granite. How could I spurn this man — and yet how, oh how, could I believe?

As I stood frozen in the white glare of his holiness, I

wondered madly what life there could be for a whore who wanted to change. Where would I go? How would I earn my bread? What wife would allow her husband to give me honest work? What other possibility was open except to go on as I had, scraping together enough money to keep myself alive until I was too old and worn to attract any but beggars? That any other choice existed for me was one I had never imagined, at least not for many years — not since, driven by desperation and despair, I had first given myself over to this life of self-denigration. Any hopes or dreams I had lay rotting under its accumulated rubble.

And now, this teacher called out to extinct hopes. I felt them stirring, revived within me, though I had thought them long dead. With the memories of hope came a stab of pain — that awful bite that comes with self-knowledge, accompanied by the misery of choice.

Perhaps that was worst of all. Wasn't my life the inevitable result of some cruel conspiracy of fate beyond my control? Once I had set my foot on the downward road there was no looking back, and none to care whether I did.

Yet here stood a man offering the possibility of choice, his intense gaze leveled at me. No one else mattered — not the priests, not the teachers of the Law, not those who had used me nor those who had abandoned me so many years ago. Only he, I, and the choice to believe or not.

That was days ago. They killed him. I was close enough to see him die — like a criminal, on a Roman death-rack. Some say he was God's son — but to die as horribly as that...

Today the crowds are gone, but a local man accosted me

in the street. "Hello, lovely," he leered, slyly jiggling his coin purse. "Care to earn a bit of silver?"

A week ago I would have beckoned him into my room without a second thought. But now I stood, caught between what I knew and what I wished to believe. The sounds of the street faded into an anonymous mumble. The only words my tongue could form were the words the rabbi had framed—

"Go...and leave your life of sin."

THE LAST TIME I saw him was in Jerusalem, at Passover-tide. He was scurrying along the Street of Potters like a furtive animal, his head down. He was muttering to himself. I called his name and he started, appearing ready to bolt. Then he recognized me.

I almost wished he hadn't. He clawed at my arm as a drowning man grasps at a rope. "Rabbi! We must tell them! We must warn them about the Nazarene!" His eyes had the glassy glare of the mad.

"What is the matter, Judas? Calm yourself, my boy, please! Yes, that's better now...come here and sit down by this wall. Now then — what troubles you so?"

He stared into the air above my head, his brow deeply furrowed, as if it required all his concentration to force the wriggling snakes of thought into shapes that words might contain. As I watched him struggle with himself, my mind drifted back...

He had been a serious child. He rarely smiled, never laughed. In lessons, when the other boys would grow restless and distracted, he remained attentive, earnestly fastening his eyes on the scrolls, striving rigidly to absorb the day's teaching.

They would tease him, call him "Old Man" or "Judas Long-Face," would bait him mercilessly. His only defenses had been tight-lipped silence, or flight.

He came to confide in me. Perhaps he sensed my pity for a child to whom mirth seemed superfluous. He knew he could talk to me without fear of ridicule. I became his friend.

"Teacher," he was saying, "there is danger on every side. This Nazarene is no ordinary insurrectionist. He is subtle, he is clever; he causes whole crowds to lose all caution! And yet...his ingenuousness can make you doubt your own judgment. He can make you think yourself wrong for being skeptical of him. Oh, he is sly! Caiaphas must be told! Something must be done!" Again the manic glitter came into his eyes; his breathing became shallow and rapid.

"Judas! Softly, my son, softly! You must not go into the presence of the Sanhedrin ranting like one possessed! Are you sure about this man? Can he truly be such a danger?"

Early in his manhood he had left Kerioth for Jerusalem. He had hoped to apprentice himself to one of the priests, to one day become a member of the Council, perhaps even high priest. In those days his ambition knew no bounds. I had smiled at his fancies, admonishing him to buy his meat one day at a time. Still I admired his resolve to meet high goals. Acquainted with his grim determination, I half believed he might one day sit among the elders. I wished him well, though I knew I would miss him. I enjoyed him; I suppose, in a way, I enjoyed his need of me.

One day, years later, he had come back, trembling with excitement. He told me Annas himself had commissioned him to be the eyes and ears of the Sanhedrin within a zealot band in Galilee. With fearful pride he swore me to silence, told me his life would be in danger if these desperate men knew his true mission. I could plainly see rapt anticipation competing with anxiety in his features. He was uncertain, yet eager to be off to meet his destiny. I had watched him go with not a little apprehension.

"I have seen things, my teacher. Things you could never..." He glanced up at the sound of approaching foot-steps. It was a juggler. I suppose the clown had seen my robes, thought we might be good for a few coppers. I was about to wave him away when Judas rose and pounced upon him, grasping him roughly by the front of his coat.

"Go away, you fool!" he hissed in the frightened stranger's face. "You're a spy, trying to hear what I'm saying! Who are you? One of Peter's zealot friends? Go tell that stinking fisher-man that Judas was too clever for you — he saw through your pitiful little ruse and sent you on your way. Hah!" With that he shoved the man backward into a stack of baskets. The poor wretch hastily gathered his colored balls, never taking his panicked eyes off Judas for more than an instant, and scurried away, looking fearfully over his shoulder as he ran.

"Fool!" muttered Judas under his breath as he glared after the juggler.

During the entire spectacle, I sat open-mouthed in shock. "Do you really think that was necessary?" I asked, astounded.

"Can you doubt it, when nothing less than the life and death of our nation is at stake? I tell you, this rebel will bring down the walls of Jerusalem on our very heads! Already the mobs chant his name in the streets! And I will tell you something else, rabbi." He looked carefully up and down the street, leaned closer to me, and said in a low voice, "He has talked of destroying *the temple.*"

One summer day, as I sat just inside the window of my house, Judas had approached, stumbling, hot and sweaty, up the dusty thoroughfare of our village. He had come straight to my door. "Teacher," he insisted as I rose to meet him, "I need to speak with you."

When the door was closed, he explained that the leader of the zealot band, a certain Jesus of Nazareth, had sent all his followers out on a recruiting mission. "He has real power. So real it is frightening — some of the things he does...But he doesn't act at all like other zealots. It was pathetically easy to infiltrate his band; indeed, he seemed to be expecting me. And though he is surrounded by men capable of violence — indeed, eager for it — he seems disinterested, even opposed to armed resistance. He spends more of his time angering the local synagogue officials than he does fomenting rebellion against Rome. I can't make sense of it."

Some months later he had returned. By this time, he had grown contemptuous of Jesus. He felt the man was weak and of no use for anything approaching armed conflict. "Not that the Sanhedrin have any intention of allowing matters to proceed that far," he had said. "He deludes those ignorant northerners. He is so equivocating, so impotent. How can they imagine he will ever be of any consequence, let alone a messiah?

"Pitiful morons," he had sneered, "who believe this Jesus is the promised one. No organization, no plan, no backing. Indeed, he even refused such support when it was offered him.

"All he will do," Judas had predicted, "is allow the blind dolts who follow him to spill their blood in a useless cause. I am sorry to see even Galilean lives wasted on this man."

I was disturbed more by the bitterness in his voice than in the judgments he was making. He seemed to be trying to convince himself.

"Yes, teacher, he must die!" Judas continued after the juggler turned a distant corner. "Oh, once I thought him weak, frail. But now I see. I understand that his is the weakness of the jackal, who waits as patiently as death for the feast following the battle!

"But," he interrupted himself — "What of the healings? What of the children, the raisings of the dead? How can such a scheming parasite be capable of such things? Unless it is a ruse, a ploy to throw me off his scent..."

He thrust his head toward me, his face a mask of insanity. "Yes, yes! That must be it! He would delude me with the appearance of holiness! But he cannot trick me that easily, no! I will go to Caiaphas and tell him."

"Judas!" I said, taking hold of his arm — "My son, wait! You are not well!"

"Let go of me! Turn me loose!" As I released my grip, I imagined the flesh falling away from his face, leaving me staring into the deep sockets of a grinning skull.

He rose and stepped away. "They will see," he said. "They will all know! Judas of Kerioth will not be forgotten..."

He turned, and rushed in the direction of the temple.

MAYBE A FEW MINUTES, maybe a couple of hours— I don't know how long I slept. But I woke to the squeaking of leather cuirasses and the click of hobnails on the stony ground. I heard the mutter of many voices, and sprang to my feet, the pounding in my chest chasing the goblins of sleep away.

He was standing quietly, facing them. He looked as if he had been wrestling Father Jacob's angel. His garment stuck to him with sweat, and weariness was etched upon his face. His eyes told a tale of some nigh-unbearable conflict raging within his soul. But he stood calmly, with perhaps a trace of apprehension, and asked them what they wanted.

I knew what they wanted. It was a lynch mob. Beneath the visors of their helmets the faces of the soldiers were hard and set, their eyes black, flickering pits of dark purpose. In the background, I saw the greedy faces of the high priest's minions, come to see their dirty work done. Jesus had been courting disaster for three years, and now it had found him. Judas stepped up to him and gave him that little kiss, so innocent, so damnable. Still he stood quietly, passively, not even raising his voice.

I'm unsure why I chose that moment to draw my sword. I caught everyone off guard, including the Romans. Before anyone knew what was happening, I had slashed off Malchus's ear. I was ready to start the holy war right then and there, I suppose. Twelve of us against at least fifty of them — not good odds, but then normal strategies never seemed to go as planned where he was concerned.

As on so many other occasions, he didn't allow matters to progress normally. He froze me in mid-stride with a word, and I turned to look at him. In his eyes I saw, of all things, pity! He pitied my ignorance, I suppose, or maybe it was my arrogance, or my fear-crazed brutality. Probably all these things. But to look at him, Malchus's blood still running down my blade, and to see not even anger, nor fear, but pity — that unnerved me more than Roman steel. My blade dropped from my numbed fingers, and I ran like a jackal into the darkness.

I could not stay away. Something drew me like a lodestone back into town, to the courtyard of Caiaphas. I saw what they had done to him, what they were doing to him. They gathered around him like hounds around a mortally wounded bear, baiting him, daring him to take the offensive, half afraid that he would. They stood with Roman bailiffs all about them, gathered in a circle around this pathetic, bleeding, hopelessly righteous man, and I swear that they feared him. That was why they were so brutal, I suppose.

♦

They were not alone in their fear. I — who have stared into the spray of a hundred storms, who have with my own hands beaten men senseless on the docks of Bethsaida — I was afraid. I knew, for all my bluster and braggadocio, that I could not do what he had done. To walk meekly into the hot, grasping hands of these fear-maddened demagogues, and to know, as I now realized he had always known, that I would die; this I could never have done. It was beyond bravery. It bordered on madness; or so I thought then.

As these half-thoughts ricocheted through my mind, a little serving girl pulled at my cloak. I suppose she noticed the way I stared into the courtyard, the way my eyes were fastened upon him. She asked me if I was one of his followers. Jerking around, I glared at her as if she had slapped me. Suddenly air became harder to pull into my lungs. Sweat broke out on my forehead and palms as I surreptitiously glanced toward the guards, hoping against hope they had not heard. Though they made no move, I could feel their hostility pointed my way, slavering as hungry wolves, eager for a new victim.

I felt the blood drain from my face. My tongue stuck to the roof of my mouth. Everyone in the courtyard seemed to close in upon me, circle me, stare at me...waiting for my answer. I could not lie, and I could not own him. I turned, knocking the girl's tray from her hands in my haste, and moved away.

But she would not let me go. She grasped at my hem, and persisted, with the idiotic tenacity of a child, in asking me if I knew him. I did not have the strength to swim against the seething current of spite I had seen in the Sanhedrin faces in the courtyard. I wished for some innocuous answer that would camouflage my fear. I caved in like a cliff undercut by too many storm tides. "No," I said, "I don't know him."

With those words, something in me died. I had been ready to take on an entire squadron singlehandedly, but now I denied him to a child. Seeing no way back, I walled myself in with the lie, and the mortar hardened. I slipped over to a small blaze kindled against the chill of the night. Someone by the fire asked me, "Aren't you one of the followers of the Nazarene? I thought I heard your northern accent." All I wanted was to huddle in my anonymity, but someone kept dragging it off me, as one might drag a piece of rotting wood off a horde of slugs.

"No, you've got it wrong. I don't know this man. You're confusing me with someone else." *Survive. Just survive. Soon something will happen. Maybe he'll start acting like a messiah, and you'll be close enough to help him. Maybe this is a dream, and when you wake up all will be well...*

Just then, they dragged him out of the courtyard, taking him to Pilate's palace. They had beaten him and cursed him, and their spittle ran down his cheeks and dripped off the end of his nose. Silence fell, as everyone looked at him with hate and curiosity. I averted my eyes, afraid and ashamed to meet his. One of the high priest's slaves happened to glance my way, then challenged me, saying "Look! Here is the fellow who cut off the ear of my cousin Malchus! He is a follower of this criminal!"

Everything stopped. There was a silence as profound as that of the tomb, stretching to infinity. I felt his gaze boring through my skull, and now I could not keep my eyes from locking with his, even as my accuser's finger was leveled at me like a dagger.

In that instant my vision changed. I saw him standing in a nimbus of purest light while the rest of us were in darkness. I was utterly repulsed by the light that cast my abject destitution into such stark relief. He beckoned to me to join him in the circle of light, but I knew that if I did, I would then be abhorred by those still in darkness. They would torture us both! They would drag us down into the blackness of Sheol! I felt the fear rising in me like an irresistible torrent. It swept my soul away in a flaming rush of panic, then spewed out of my mouth in noisome curses and denial of the light. Darkness was speaking through me, cursing him, and I was its willing instrument! The wolves were baying at my heels, and I was feeding him to them instead. *No, spare me! Here, you want him, not me! Take him! Take him! I'll give you anything, only spare me!* And then a rooster crowed.

He looked at me as though I had just driven the nails into his hands. Now there was no vision, no light; only a wounded, grieving man. Grieving — for whom? I remembered what he had prophesied as we gathered around the Seder earlier that evening. Yes, he had known all along that I, too, would curse him and spit on him, and now he was there, blood oozing from the raw meat of his back, grieving for *me!* A sob burst from my throat and I turned and ran again, racing into the dark alleyways like a whipped cur.

I didn't go out at all for the next three days. But thoughts stampeded through my mind like jittery beasts, following each other in a circling, manic parade. Recalling my denial of him at the high priest's house, it came to me that I had spoken

♦

more truly than I realized. I wondered if any of the twelve of us had ever really known. I thought about our dreams of Messiah. As boys, Andrew and I had imagined ourselves as His lieutenants, fighting the infidels and reclaiming David's throne. How we had imagined ourselves as terrible engines of God's wrath, avenging the wrongs done to the children of Israel.

Then along came this man, and surely, we thought, this was He! Who else could heal lepers or cast out demons or raise the dead? The One was come. The time had arrived! Now God would seat this heir of David on the White Throne, and we — *we* would judge the nations!

But he refused the role we had imputed to him. He steadfastly set his face toward a hideous, needless death, and now his wish was granted. I knew what was happening as surely as if I was seeing it with my own eyes.

He was being slain on the Sanhedrin's altar, condemned by a Roman magistrate to the death of a murderer or thief. He was at once a sop to the fickle mob and a bloody token the Sanhedrin could display as proof of their desperate hold on a semblance of power. Their rabid jealousy of him was the only thing stronger than their hatred of the Romans. I had seen the bloodthirsty stare of the monster, felt its fetid breath on my face, and allowed him to be sucked into its maw alone, unaided, friendless. How could I go and witness his mangling? I stayed hidden, pulling my stinking cloak of broken dreams close around me, until just before dawn following the Sabbath.

At first I thought Mary's sanity had been overpowered by her grief. Then I recalled something about a temple destroyed but rebuilt in three days. John and I looked at each other for a moment. The next thing I knew we were bolting out the door.

We didn't find him there, of course. I went right into the tomb — folded grave clothes and dried aloe leaves lay on the slab. There was no smell of death, an odor indisguisable, even when cloaked in spices and perfumes.

On the way home I tried to quench my kindled hopes. Grave robbers, I thought. Or else some subterfuge of the Sanhedrin, meant to further humiliate and intimidate any who might be contemplating rallying around his banner. I was not sure which I feared most: that it was true or that it was false. Suppose Mary really had seen him? If he was, somehow, impossibly, alive again, it could only mean that he had a power beyond all imagining. And I had betrayed him, as surely as did Judas. What would he say to me? What justice would he mete upon me? I was not ready to face him, should he be alive.

And then He Himself was among us. All my uncertainties, all my postulates, all my points of reference were in an instant swept away by the sight of Him, not just alive again, but *more* alive than ever, more alive than I! As if the sun came down from the sky and stood among the tallow lamps, so it was when He came among us. I stayed back, transfixed. I wanted to look Him in the eye, to embrace Him...and I wanted to hide my face, to escape His impossible, terrifying Presence.

The second time He came, I watched belief bursting across Thomas's face as he saw the wounds in His hands and side. I looked on in envy as Thomas knelt at His feet, doubt melting away like frost on a spring morning. Then I heard from somewhere the wretched echo of a rooster crowing, and I could not move.

But the third time was different. Several of us had gone fishing. I suppose we were trying to assimilate the bewildering new universe in which we found ourselves by going back to the old familiar patterns. We would fish awhile, then talk awhile, trying to reason it through, trying to comprehend even a small corner of this mystery in which we were caught. It was good that we had each other to talk to, because the fishing was terrible. We worked the nets all night without success.

Toward dawn we were approaching the shore when a man walking along the beach called out. He asked if we had caught anything, and we groused about our awful luck, as fishermen will do. He advised us to try another cast. Having nothing better to do, we dropped the nets over the side one more time, and all the fish of Galilee tried to get in.

I felt the flesh prickle in bumps along my arms. Someone — I think it was John — said, "It's Him." I knew he was right. The power flowed from the man, though He stood a good stone's throw from where we were. Spontaneously I decided to go to Him, to seek forgiveness or death. Before I could change my mind, I dove, fully clothed, into the sea and swam to shore.

By the time I got there He had a fire going and asked for some fish. My tongue was tied. I could not look at Him. All I could think about were things I wanted to say to Him, yet could not force from my throat for the shame I felt.

He said nothing to me until the others had arrived and we had finished eating. Then, as we wiped our hands on our robes and tossed the bones into the fire, He looked at me and said, "Simon, do you love Me?"

Slowly, slowly I raised my eyes to His, expecting perhaps to see anger and rebuke, expecting to be embarrassed in front of my friends. Instead, the love in His gaze blinded me to anyone but Him. There was a long pause, as He continued boring in on my soul.

"Lord," I stammered finally, "You know I love You!" I wanted to tell Him that I was sorry, that I hated myself for lying about Him. I wanted to confess that I was a weak man whose pride outraced his judgment. I wanted to cry aloud, to beat my breast, to spill my sins before Him and gain His pardon. I could not do or say any of these things. I could only look into His eyes and know that He already knew. But again came His gently framed question: "Simon Peter, do you love Me?"

"Lord, I have told You. I have no other words. You know I love You." The question ripped through my bowels like twin knives.

Then again: "Simon, do you love Me?" Three questions, as brutal as those three asked of me that night in the court-yard. If I had possessed a blade, at that moment I would have plunged it into my heart. Tried and convicted by my own con-science, I would willingly have carried out the sentence. Only the scintillating force of His gaze held me. I answered Him again, my voice coming from a distance as great as the darkness between the stars: "Lord, You know I love You."

Sometimes when all is quiet, I can still remember His eyes, holding me captive with forgiveness, setting me free with scalding, healing love as He posed the questions whose answers He knew — and so cleansed my wound and laved my heart in His light.

Lord...You know I love You...

Journal

T HIS EVENING as I write my daily account, I am disquieted almost beyond telling. Jesus, the rabbi from the northern district whom we have been investigating, came to Jerusalem today, riding an ass and causing an uncalledfor display of frenzy among the masses. Who can say when these aroused young hotheads will bring down the wrath of Rome upon us all? Even Shemaiah, my own grandson, who makes a child's mouthings about casting the legionary eagle out of Jerusalem, went out to cheer the man's entrance. It is frightening to contemplate what might happen to us all if one of these zealot movements should prove too troublesome. I know, as surely as I am Gamaliel, that if intervention comes, Rome will make no fine distinctions between Jews.

I watch and wait. I pray the Eternal God will grant us wisdom to navigate the shoals lying before us, for this land is a seething cauldron of cross-purposes.

✡ "Give Caesar what is Caesar's, and give God what is God's" — that's what I heard the Galilean teacher say today, and the words won't leave my mind. I have no great love for Caesar, but I abide by the laws and offer the prescribed sacrifices for his health, and of course I am righteous in observing the law. What does that teacher mean?

✡ Tumult clutches Jerusalem! This Galilean created a stir beyond anything in memory. I heard him ranting as that mad son of Zechariah's used to do. He wreaked havoc in the temple grounds, railing against the merchants of sacrificial animals and the currency changers. He called them thieves and drove them bodily out of the temple. The crowds listened with rowdy delight as he spoke to the scribes and elders as to unwashed peasants. At least the Baptist confined his raucous shouting to the Jordan wilderness. But this fellow comes boldly into our temple!

If possible, he has even less appreciation than John did of political realities. John, in fact, articulated things we were all thinking — I couldn't help chuckling into my hand at the expression Herod wore when the wild man from the wilderness publicly accosted him for his harlot bride.

But the Nazarene! I can tell he has an impressive command of the Torah, yet the arguments he draws from it run completely counterpoint. He quoted Moses as though he were preaching to infidels instead of guardians of the covenant of Abraham! And the rabble are incited by his every word. I am alarmed, as are all the Sanhedrin, by the riotous emotions he arouses in the masses, the open contempt he exhibits for our delicate position. Clearly something must be done to restore order and keep Rome from storming in.

✡ This day we put the Nazarene to death. Peculiar to relate, the peasants who scant days earlier had shouted "Hosanna!" and laid palm branches at his feet today turned against him in Pilate's courtyard, screaming for his blood. We had feared the crowds, it seems, for no reason. How easy to persuade them against this would-be messiah! Thus it is with a mob; a stupid beast with many throats and no head.

I had expected quite a different performance from the man. For one who had boldly declaimed against the elders of his people, today he was oddly muted before the Council. I had the disquieting impression he held his tongue not for dread nor the absence of support from the multitudes, but because of some inner calm which had little to do with us. He seemed uncowed, despite his perplexing silence. There were moments when I felt that I was on trial, not he; that I was weighed in *his* balances.

But enough. He is slain, and his followers are in hiding — if, indeed, there are any followers left. Surely the curse of death on a tree will drive from their deluded minds any notion of his being the messiah. The sooner this commotion is forgotten the better.

Distasteful though the business was, it is done, and for the best.

✡ Today I had occasion to speak with Samuel, Shemaiah's tutor. He says that the young man does well, and I am not surprised. From his early childhood he has shown a certain precocity in his yearning for knowledge. Indeed, Samuel finds no fault in my grandson's discipline nor his preparation. Shemaiah seems in almost every way a dedicated and eager student.

And yet, I sense from the tone of my old friend Samuel's remarks that Shemaiah is, sometimes, *too* zealous in his search for understanding. Indeed, he could perhaps be considered by some as impertinent in his persistent questioning, his unbridled determination to know the *why* behind every premise. It is a trait I have seen in the boy myself, and chose to overlook. I must take a personal interest in his education. Some subtlety is required to channel his impetuosity without creating a docile hack or a sullen rebel. In fact, the boy reminds me of a particular student of mine. A brilliant mind he has, but he lacks a certain restraint, a certain recognition of the necessity for maturity. I will watch Shemaiah carefully and judge what might be done with him.

✡ This Nazarene business refuses to fade! Yesterday, one of his disciples, an ignorant fisherman from the north, clambered up before a host of Jews from all corners of the empire and proclaimed not only that the man was no longer dead, but — incredibly — that the Eternal had raised him to sit at His right hand, anointing him Lord!

Even more astounding, I saw hundreds who actually seemed to believe this madness. They underwent proselytic bathing in the name of Jesus! What logic can possibly avail against such mass lunacy?

Jerusalem could become a staging ground for general revolt, but rebellion seems irrelevant to the intentions of these peasant preachers. They encourage people only to believe in their Jesus as the Son of the Most High, and receive washing in His name. Their converts are instructed to renounce sin and devote themselves to prayer and study of the Scriptures.

These northerners, though unlearned and untrained, are persuading entire masses to renounce the sane interpretations codified in the *Mishnah* in favor of some new doctrine with nothing to commend it save the circumstantial evidence of an empty tomb. What power drives these men?

✡ Each day some disciples of Jesus can be found in the temple courts, proclaiming to any who will listen the supposed resurrection of this one they name Messiah. These Nazarenes seem benign enough; they break no laws, instigate no riots, create no disturbances. Yet I am ill at ease with their presence in Jerusalem, their steadily increasing numbers.

How can a dead messiah save our nation? Pretenders to David's throne have always vaunted themselves, only to be utterly crushed. How long until Tiberius wearies of our pretension to kingdom and comes in force against us? Will the Eternal, blessed be He, once again allow our dispersion, as in the days of the Assyrians and Babylonians? One of my students evinces a similar discomfort. He chafes at the Sanhedrin's inaction. He is young; perhaps he will learn patience with age.

✡ Yesterday we heard for ourselves what these followers of the Galilean have to say. One of their leaders, the fisherman called Simon by some and Peter by others, somehow healed a lame beggar at the temple gate. Inevitably a crowd gathered,

and Peter, accompanied by one John, also a fisherman from
Bethsaida, began preaching to the people, crediting Jesus of
Nazareth for the miracle.

They accused the Sanhedrin of ignorance in the case of
Jesus, saying we put him to death because we failed to recognize his true identity. Were the churls attempting to be
gracious? Their remarks were hardly interpreted in that light!
We arrested them, holding them over until this morning, when
the Council convened to judge their case.

If we thought they would be abashed and tongue-tied
standing before the supreme judges of Israel, we were greatly
mistaken. Never have I seen a demeanor as fiery as that of
Simon of Bethsaida! These simple men were uncomfortably
reminiscent of the Nazarene himself, boldly proclaiming their
allegiance to the Eternal, their avowal of his power through
his son. They quoted David, as if to claim him as one of their
own as well.

We were caught in an awkward pose. We could not deny
the fact of the healing, for the invalid was widely known to all
who frequented the temple district. The city buzzed with talk
of the incident. What could we do? Punish them for doing a
good deed? We sternly commanded them to stop preaching
about their Jesus. We might have saved our breath.

I wonder at their brazen courage. What zealot ever made
a lame man walk, or dared bring such indictments before the
Sanhedrin? Their fervor is of another order, one I fail to grasp.

✡ My grandson's behavior alarms me. I don't know the
source of the troubling ideas in his head, but I'm apprehensive
about where they will lead him. Shemaiah suggests terrible,

almost blasphemous things about the high priest and his family; contemptuous of Rome, he chafes at any notion of restraint. He acts as though we are engaged in some facile exercise in right and wrong — complexities and considerations of expediency simply do not exist for him. He has no understanding of the difficulties faced daily by the Sanhedrin — the strain of preserving our identity as a people while avoiding the unwelcome attentions of Caesar; the constant attempts at placation, at keeping both the Zealots and the legions at bay.

Today he told me he despises the men mumbling into their beards, nodding over the Torah, while all around them the nation lies prostrate for godless, bloody Romans — "the wolf bitch's sucklings," he called them. He flung his words like stones, and each one struck me.

I remember when I, also, burned with certainties, when I first felt the hot desire for the will of the Eternal. Shemaiah's anger reminds me of those days when answers flamed on my tongue, quick, naive. I love Shemaiah's desire for purity, for clear choices. I admire his zeal for holiness.

What happened to the passion I once felt? Was it broken by the weight of responsibility and the seduction of prestige?

But the thoughts created by the shock of hateful words from the lips of my own flesh and blood are better left in the dim half-light.

✿ I continue to think of Shemaiah and his fire. Each day brings its own urgency, I have decided, and I have no will for passion now. Where passion rules, reason languishes. Shemaiah could never accept this.

May Yahweh grant that such men never rule in Judea, for then we are lost.

✡ Today all twelve leaders of the Nazarene sect were before the Council. Caiaphas and his advisers hate them the more deeply because they espouse, as we Pharisees do, the resurrection of the dead. Indeed, their peculiar creed is founded upon it.

I mistrust this dangerous reliance upon the resurrection of a man I saw nailed to a cross, pierced by a Roman lance. Surely it is folly to place an irrevocable belief in one who made extravagant claims for himself during life, yet died ignobly.

Still, I cannot explain the unaccountable conviction of these men. If they led an armed band, I would expect a certain amount of swagger, but they give not the slightest hint of military or political ambition. They simply, unequivocally refuse to deny the power of their Christ or to stop preaching in his name.

I was reminded, listening to these bold peasants, of something Jesus once said that I had hoped to forget. When he denounced us for binding laws upon our people, laws not motivated by mercy, love, and mutual respect, I couldn't help remembering the prophet Ezekiel's message of woe for those shepherds of Israel who slaughter the flock to fill their own bellies.

I will not deny it; these men and their incomprehensible fervor roil the waters of my soul. I cannot escape being impressed by their message, despite my attempts to reason with myself. Caiaphas claims we should put them to death, lest they spawn rebellion and cause Rome to raze the temple. Perhaps the high priest is right. Perhaps not.

My ambivalence found voice at the trial of these "apostles," as they name themselves. Gazing around the council chamber, I saw different tales scribed upon the faces of the Sanhedrin. I saw naked hate displayed boldly on the features of Annas and Caiaphas. Sympathy, perhaps even commiseration, glimmered in the eyes of Nicodemus and one or two others. But confusion was written on most countenances, akin to that in my own heart.

The Sadducees made no secret of their desire to kill the Nazarenes out of hand, but I counseled against such a precipitous act despite my misgivings. I reminded them of the false messiahs arisen over the past decades, all of whom came, soon or late, to the point of the sword. I believe the wiser course is to release these men, to leave them to the judgment of the Eternal, lest we, all unknowing, be found contending against Him. As I spoke, Nicodemus drew a relieved sigh. My student, Saul, observing in the shadows behind the council seats, clenched his jaw and turned away.

✡ Shemaiah has joined a zealot band. I am grieved to the soul that such folly should be perpetrated by my own flesh. I find myself thinking that, if he were to abandon our beliefs, I would rather have him join the Nazarenes than the zealots. But, of course, when the Galilean submitted to Pilate and a cross, Shemaiah lost all respect for him.

The zealots are lauded by simple country folk, but these bandits will bring only destruction upon Jerusalem. They practice petty harassment upon the legions and assassinate any Hebrews whom they judge to be cozy with Rome. They win the plaudits of fools, but make the middle course we would steer ever narrower and more perilous. Inflamed by the memory of the Maccabees, they are, in truth, rabid dogs. Thinking of my grandson among such rabble is more than I can bear.

✡ My brilliant student Saul has become the scourge of the Nazarenes, pursuing them from house to house to bring them to trial. What zeal drives him to become a coursing hound?

A few days ago, a certain Stephen was arraigned before us on charges that seemed suspect to me. However he came to be there, he castigated us, calling us prophet-slayers, unclean, lawbreakers. The consequent outpouring of hate was sudden and absolute. The man was washed away on a torrent of loathing, murdered outside the city gate with Saul leading the way. I hobbled along behind in time to hear Stephen's last utterance — the same helpless plea as his master's: "Lord, forgive them..."

The Nazarenes are deserting the city in droves. But from what I have witnessed, getting them out of Jerusalem will hardly lessen their impact. As the wind from a fire seeds the dry grasses with sparks, so I expect their expulsion will serve only to salt the earth with their ardency. Wherever they go, they will speak of their Messiah.

Daily I ponder the fervent faith of those who worship the slain Jesus. I have failed to fathom the source of its vitality. It cannot arise merely from the minds of men. Something that is more than human empowers the wonders done by these believers. And when did Satan ever bring healing?

Throughout history, we Jews have been a people of strange beginnings, unlikely heroes. From the dry loins of Father Abraham and the ancient, barren womb of Sarah, the Eternal drew forth Isaac, the sire of Israel. And Joseph...that coddled young son of Jacob's old age, went about with his head in the clouds, foolishly drawing to himself the hatred of his brethren, yet he sustained Israel in Egypt during famine. What of Moses, the great lawgiver? Only after fleeing the court of Pharaoh and spending the prime of his life as a goatherd in Midian did he become the mighty prophet leading Israel to Canaan. And Gideon? He was the last son of the weakest house of Manasseh. Our great king David, anointed by Samuel, was the youngest and least favored of Jesse's sons, and was forced to live like a bandit in the desert while waiting for his reign to begin.

✡   This Sabbath past, I attended a meeting of the Nazarenes with Nicodemus. I kept my face hidden and sat in the shadows, for I felt my open presence would foster suspicion. Nicodemus, apparently, regularly and unpretentiously attends the gatherings. In fact, I recognized several priests among their number.

They assemble late on the Sabbath, continuing their worship into the first day of the week, the day of their Messiah's resurrection. There is nothing adverse about their worship; they read from the Torah and the Prophets, sing Psalms, pray, and receive teaching. But each act is suffused, impregnated with the name of the dead rabbi, Jesus.

They make a habit of taking bread and the after-supper cup from the Seder in memory of the crucified one. They claim this act was commanded by him on the very night he was betrayed by that follower of his from Kerioth. Avowing their master's exaltation to the right hand of God, they pledge mutual support in the exchange of bread and wine.

The so-called apostles lead them, exerting authority in teaching, in disputes, in spiritual discernment. But that which commends itself most to me is the manner of loving submission among these people. One can almost believe, after observing them, that they truly know the Holy One.

Recently Herod put one of their apostles, a certain James from Bethsaida, to the sword. But rather than rising up in vengeance, these believers offered praise to the Eternal for receiving the soul of James, and for counting them worthy to suffer persecution for the name of Jesus the Anointed. This, such a radical change from the bilious gall spouted between the clenched teeth of the zealots!

During the meeting, one of the believers read aloud a letter from another of their brethren in Rome. Many Greek-speaking Jews who left Jerusalem under the threats of Saul persuade numbers of their new home synagogues throughout the Dispersion to take the name of Jesus of Nazareth. Despite violent efforts to eradicate it, the seed prospers.

✡ We have received reports that Saul, arch-enemy of the Nazarenes, joins their number! It is said he claims to have seen with his own eyes the risen person of Jesus.

I was aware that he had petitioned Caiaphas for writs permitting him to seize Damascene followers of Jesus. Naturally, the Sadducees were only too happy to grant his wish. On his way to Damascus, the tale now runs, Saul was smitten by a brilliant light and struck blind. He continued into the city, where he was actually visited by a local leader of the Nazarenes. This man allegedly healed Saul's eyesight. Now Saul is himself preaching the resurrection of Jesus, debating actively in the synagogues, and arguing vigorously that this Galilean was the Messiah.

What alchemy could possibly have transposed Saul's venom? Upon whose forge was the metal of his soul remolded into this radically different cast? I, who knew Saul so well, would be no more stunned if told that a zealot leader had journeyed to Rome in sackcloth and kissed the feet of Claudius.

Transforming Saul's heart from unswerving hatred of the believers to passionate belief in their Messiah is not, to my mind, in the hand of man. This thing has about it the fragrance of the Eternal.

✡ Nicodemus tells me the way of Jesus is now being preached to the Gentiles. The word finds acceptance with many of the God-fearers, as well as with unwashed pagans who, seeing the miracles wrought by the evangelists, are moved to worship. Is fellowship between the children of Abraham and the uncircumcised nations possible? How can those who are unclean be made clean? How shall the hand of the Eternal rest upon those who have not the Law? I find myself adrift in a sea of uncertainty. Scarcely have I found sure mooring since first I encountered the Nazarene, years ago.

✡ Could this union of Jew and Gentile possibly be the fulfillment of Isaiah's prophecy? Could this crucified one be that root of Jesse who will stand as an ensign to the nations? Is it he whom all the peoples shall seek?

✡ Today I have wrestled with this question: How could a messiah be crucified? Prophetic tradition teaches us that Messiah shall rule, shall re-establish David's throne, shall be a warrior before whom no prince, no king, no power prevails. Messiah shall never die, nor His kingdom fade. Nothing shall deter His eternal reign over Israel's lives and hearts.

And yet, is this not the very thing occurring with these impossibly committed Nazarenes? Their faith is a madness, a stumbling block, but still their numbers swell, encompassing even Gentiles whose fathers never knew the Eternal.

Suppose, just for a moment: If this resurrection be true, could this possibly be the very thing of which David spoke, saying, "Thou shalt not let Thy Holy One see decay?" And was not the behavior of the Nazarene before us, his accusers, like that spoken of in Isaiah: "He was oppressed and afflicted, yet he opened not his mouth"?

Like Moses, I may be treading unwittingly upon holy ground.

✡ I had prayed never to see Shemaiah's face again, but I cannot shut away my grandson's heart. And today I received this letter from him:

"Beloved Grandfather: I know you disapprove of what I'm doing. I don't expect to make you agree with me — but I want you to at least understand my devotion to the Cause. I tried talking to Father, but he won't listen to me or see me. I only hope you will read this and know my motivation.

"The Lord promised this land to our people. He gave it to Father Abraham as an eternal inheritance. True, our fathers sinned, forgetting to seek the Lord. But He brought them back, out of Persia, out of pagan lands, and helped them rebuild Jerusalem as a monument to His steadfast love and power. Kings have come and gone, but Jerusalem remains.

"Now the fist of Rome tightens about our throats. It is time for the Lord to place His hand on one among us, to raise up a champion from among the seed of David. We don't know when He will do this, but we believe the prophets teach the inevitable coming of Messiah, and we want to be ready when the day arrives. We shall be His army, placing ourselves eagerly in His command to cleanse the land of our fathers from all unrighteousness.

"This is our aim, Grandfather: To work the will of the Lord when He moves against the infidel, as He promised through His prophets. We are not highwaymen, waylaying innocent travelers for gold. We hold ourselves in constant readiness for the battle summons of Messiah. We stringently observe the Law, that we might be pure in the sight of our General.

"Grandfather, my earliest memories are of being with you and Father, listening as you studied and discussed the Torah. I well remember my boyish pride in being the son and grandson of teachers of the Law. I dreamed of the day when I, too, should wear the vestments and serve in the temple on the High Days of the Lord.

"But how can I worship the Holy God on an altar dependent for its existence on the whim of this deluded emperor who claims godhood? I am sickened by the fawning compromises practiced by Annas and his sons to retain their offices.

The influence of their sin pollutes even the Temple, making an obscene mockery of the sons of Levi. I will have no dealings with men who corrupt the Law with their left hand while judging Israel with the right. In your deepest heart, surely you must feel the same sense of shame.

"Please understand, dear Grandfather: My love for the Torah drove me into Eleazar's band. I harbor no contempt for you or Father. I tread this path because the Lord of Hosts compels me.

"I do not expect your blessing, nor even your reply. Greet my father. I beseech the Lord each day for him, as I do for you. May He hold up your arms. May He bless Israel, and hasten the coming Day of Messiah."

Shemaiah is right: He does not make me agree with him or approve of his involvement with the bandits. In fact, I fear for him all the more, and this evening found myself weeping for him — and for us all.

✡ Word comes of a great burning in Rome — the entire city engulfed in flames, thousands dead. Immediately, the report goes, Nero began rebuilding the city from smoldering ashes.

Some placed the blame for the conflagration on the followers of Jesus who live there. Their prophecies tell of a great fire which will consume the whole earth, and many interpret this calamity as their attempt to hasten the day.

I dislike this construction of circumstance. I have seen nothing in these people that hints at their desire for anarchy, or abetment of it. When their leaders are executed, they worship the Eternal and petition Him to forgive the murderers!

✡ Plenty enough Romans must believe the tale about the Nazarenes' responsibility in burning Rome, for we hear that the lives of the Nazarenes there and everywhere are made excruciating. Persecution against them has arisen throughout the empire. One hears rumors of ghastly depredations practiced upon them by Nero...too appalling to contemplate.

But does the Emperor's systematic extermination retard the propagation of their faith? Hardly. With all the might of Rome arrayed against them — their leaders either dead or fugitives, their people being boiled alive or hunted by wild beasts — still they proclaim the divinity of Jesus, and call upon Him for deliverance, if not from Nero, then from this world's wounds. The emperor will be no more able to quench their zeal than was the Sanhedrin a score and a half years ago. And history will judge him, like us, the harsher for having made the attempt.

✡ Today I thought this: If I could stand in the Roman palace, before the very throne, and prophesy, I would say: "No man can withstand the hand of the Eternal. Oh yes, *Princeps,* you too are but flesh. Once, long ago, we attempted to suppress the followers of Jesus the Nazarene and their belief. But God willed that they should not be silenced. Our people have learned, through weary ages with myriad painful stripes, that His aims may not be circumvented. Still, some of us fail to heed His teaching. We shall suffer the same fate as you, O Nero, for presuming to speak in the place of Him Who Is."

✡ Judea and Galilee are in open revolt against Rome. Brothers slay brothers in the city streets, armed bands occupy the strongholds of Masada and Antonia, and Nero is sending Vespasian at the head of a legion to put a violent halt to the insurrection. I had earnestly hoped I would not live to see this day.

The trouble began when Florus, Caesar's procurator, proceeded with his extortions to the extremity of garnishing monies for the imperial tribute from the temple treasury. Certainly this sacrilege could not be borne, but before calmer voices could prevail, rioting erupted, blood spilled...and the die is cast.

✡ Three rival camps of rebel leaders now war with each other in Jerusalem for supremacy, as though Rome were an insufficient adversary. The zealots march about and crow stridently. They invoke the name of the Eternal as though it were a talisman against the bloody fate awaiting them. Thankfully, Shemaiah's band has ensconced itself at Masada, so he is at least spared the curse of kin-slaying.

Meanwhile, Vespasian methodically reduces the northern districts; it cannot be long before he focuses his attention here.

My prayers go up by night and day for the holy city. I beg the Eternal to spare her and not lay the sins of her children to her charge. When Vespasian comes to Zion, he will leave no stone atop another. He will ransack the temple. Our nation shall cease to be.

May the Eternal smite me with blindness, that I might not witness her humiliation. O, Jerusalem! The wells of my soul run dry from grief for your tribulation.

✡ When I was young, all the world seemed to me one promise of sweetness. Each sunrise bore on its breast a rosy blessedness, mine for the taking. The Eternal was near, His will lucid. His face smiled upon my days.

Now an old man, my days are bitter. I have seen more dying than one man should be allowed to witness. I have mourned for the city of the King. I have suffered the death of my grandson. My eyes are emptied of tears, yet my heart continues to break.

Shemaiah managed to smuggle a letter out to me before the end. Three days passed before I summoned the strength to have it read to me. Reassuring me of his love for his father and me, he recounted his devotion to the land and the Law. He told me of their covenant: that not one of them — man, woman or child — should live to be taken by the Romans. I wonder if they, too, died asking forgiveness for their enemies?

I have been witness to the growth of two causes. I saw that the followers of both were equally convinced of divine charter, and willing to die for their vision. Yet one reaches beyond our nation, our time, and thrives in the fires of persecution; the other perishes in the desert.

A bitter cup to swallow, this business. Shall it ever be thus, O Eternal, our God? Will You forever demand the blood of one as the price of life for another? When comes an end to the dying?

O Nazarene...does the answer lie in Your wounded hand?

Eulogy

K YROPHILON, to Gaius, my beloved elder brother in the faith: Greetings in the Lord to you and those with you whom the Father has blessed.

Each day those of us remaining here yearn for your presence and your wise counsel, yet we believe and know that the brethren there continually thank our Lord and Savior for your love and guidance.

I fear more each day for the future of our brethren. The old one grows weaker from moment to moment. I cannot help thinking that our Lord, lacking his companionship, is now calling him to be by His side forever. What shall we do when he leaves us? I believe he, too, frets about this; indeed his concern for the followers of the Way seems the only tether binding him to this world.

The hardest thing to see, dear Gaius, is the inexorable slipping away of his mind. Day by day he sits in his small cell dictating letters. Those of us who attend him dread dispatching these, for fear that the recipients will have cause to sneer. Yesterday, as I waited upon him in his chamber, he bade me take up pen and parchment. From his lips feebly stumbled the same simple phrases, repeated, inverted and reiterated in retrograde. Sometimes as he spoke he stopped, staring into blank space for long periods of time, as though someone just around an invisible corner whispered messages in a secret language.

My heart breaks watching the madness take him. To remember him as he was in my boyhood — firm, clear-eyed, with a vigor belying his years — and to behold him now, old, weary, and distracted…I bear it poorly.

For days on end he sits, staring pensively out over the sea, brooding and mumbling to no one. He insists we bring him any reports received from the brethren abroad. This practice surely will prove his final undoing. You must remember how deeply his heart was smitten when Diotrephes spurned him. He is far weaker now than then, my brother. We know not when he may hear some dire tiding that causes him to utterly despair of this life. We fear it at any time.

I beg you, Gaius, to complete your task there as soon as may be, and come back to us. We covet your return, and I believe it would much comfort the beloved one to embrace you once again. Your friendship is a firm anchor for each of us, but he, above all, needs the blessing I know you would bring.

Greet the brothers and sisters in Crete. Lysander and Eumenides send salutation. Demetria and her household pray daily for your safety, as do we all.

May our God speed your journey home.

THEON the Younger, deacon of the assembly at Philadelphia:
To Kyrophilon, servant of the Lord Jesus Christ.

Greetings to you and those with you who share our blessed faith.

I pray most earnestly that it goes well for the Beloved One. Many of us here cherish the elder brother whom you serve faithfully. Indeed, we regard him as a treasure most precious, for he is the last of those whose eyes beheld the face of our Lord and Savior.

In truth, I write to you for the purpose of healing a wound that should never have been inflicted. Our dear bishop Diotrephes, who bears daily the burden of stewardship for the saints here, is aggrieved by the schism between himself and Brother John, though he scarcely knows how to begin the mending.

I know his heart, Kyrophilon; he would be greatly comforted believing he and John might be reconciled once again. But he is sometimes a proud man, and the gravity with which he regards his responsibility can make him more quick-tongued than he would wish.

He truly loves Brother John, I say to you, and has never ceased loving him despite the sharp exchange of words at their last meeting. I believe he has regretted, time and again, that moment of carelessness; in his heart he has retracted his harshness a thousand times over.

Will you not speak to John, my brother? Will you not ease the way for breaking down the wall separating these two great servants of our Lord? I feel sure Diotrephes would gladly seek agreement with him, were he but slightly hopeful of the successful conclusion of the matter. Let us be peacemakers, you and I. Did not our Lord pronounce a blessing on such ones?

I await your reply with prayer.

May the love of Christ and the grace of God the Father bless your spirit.

KYROPHILON to Gaius: Greetings.

I pray this letter reaches you with all possible dispatch. Our beloved old one departs soon. The circumstances of his imminent death are remarkable, but you may rely on my solemn oath before God Almighty as to the veracity of what I now relate.

It is now four Lord's Days since you left us for Ephesus. On the last Lord's Day but one I went to Brother John's room at sunrise, as was my custom, to assist him in preparing for our memorial feast. When I reached his quarters I found the door closed and locked against me. Alarmed, I called out to him and pounded on the door.

As I paused, listening, I heard him cry out — whether in fear or adoration, I do not know. I ran out and around to his window. He sat at his table, bent assiduously over a haphazard pile of parchment, writing at a furious pace. His eyes were focused maniacally on his work, and his face was drawn into a rictus of awful urgency. I spoke loudly to him several times, but may as well have addressed the waves crashing on the rocks below. I went away trembling with apprehension, and told the others.

For three days we stood vigil as he labored unceasingly. None dared attempt entry. We placed food in baskets lowered through the window, but it went untouched. He neither halted

nor paused for rest, stopping not even for darkness: He wrote
through the night as in daylight, without so much as a single
candle by which to see.

You may imagine our trepidation, dear Gaius. It was plain
that some divine message gripped him. We heard him shout
snatches of what seemed to be visions veiled to all but him,
and none of us knew when these might overpower his spirit,
shattering him as we watched helplessly.

At last, toward evening of the third day, he fell forward
onto the table. Fearing the worst, I leapt through the window.
Seeing that he lived, I beckoned to Flavius, who likewise
bounded into the room. We carried him to his couch and
attempted to arrange him comfortably. Presently his breathing
slowed and deepened, and we could see he slept.

Flavius motioned me to the table. He held several sheets
of the parchment, gazing from them to me with a strange
expression. I took one of the sheets: This aged, infirm, seem-
ingly deranged man had written in a hand as strong and clear
as any trained *emanuensis*. The entire folio was inscribed in
the same manner.

When Brother John finally awoke, we anxiously inquired
about his well-being. He reassured us that his vision had done
him no harm, but warned us he would soon be leaving. We
doubted not for a moment his meaning. His face, even as we
wait, shines with the afterglow of a light not meant for this
earth, and his eyes restlessly seek somewhere beyond.

I write this to you that you might return and speak to him
for the last time. There can be no question: The old one soon
sleeps in the arms of the Shepherd. May God grant wings to
your feet, that you may arrive before it is too late.

DIOTREPHES, bishop of the disciples at Philadelphia, to John, apostle of our Lord Jesus Christ, worthy servant of God Most High and dearest brother to us all:

Greetings in the Lord.

You must know that a great sadness has dragged at my heart since our last, ill-fated meeting. Many times I have recollected those moments of anger and many times I have desired to recall them, to live them differently and give a more worthy accounting of myself. I am deeply sorry for the hurtful words I inflicted upon you, words you did not deserve, and which I remember only with shame.

Who am I to speak to you of burdens? Who has borne a heavier load than you, the last apostle? And yet, in no other way can I explain the anxiety, the awful sense of responsibility I feel for my flock here. I blamed this burden of duty for my lack of tolerance — but such a lapse can never be excused, only pardoned.

I offer no plea other than a confession of my own weakness; I ask no concession other than an assurance of your continued love and fellowship. I spurned you, my beloved elder brother, out of a misguided notion of protection for my congregation. May God forgive me; I thought I knew better than you what their needs were. I forgot, in that cursed moment, that our Lord's last prayer was for love to reign among His children. I faced the choice to love or to demand, and to my disgrace I chose the latter. I was drunk with the wine of authority. I forgot the path to the throne lies through the slave's quarters.

The bishop's mantle lies heavily on my shoulders, Brother

John. I covet your counsel and your wisdom. Please say it is not too late for us to embrace once again.

May God speed this letter to you, and may He grant that we will once again share the sweet fellowship we once enjoyed.

Before God Himself, such is my earnest hope.

GAIUS, a servant of the Lord, to Diotrephes, bishop of Philadelphia:

I pray God's richest blessings on you, brother, and on the saints for whom He has made you overseer.

Our beloved elder brother, John, the apostle of Christ, has gone to be with his Lord. He died before receiving your letter. His final task accomplished, he was at last able to lay down the yoke of this life and pass on to the reward he so richly deserved.

We should not weep for him, Diotrephes. And if we must weep, let tears of joy anoint his passing; for through this beloved apostle, the Lord Jesus Christ has left each of us — you, me, and a myriad other saints — a living monument, a eulogy to the world.

Let John's memory be a sweet incense, a perfume evoking the love you shared which binds even beyond the grave.

Never forget that love, my brother. Never, never forget.